The
FIFTH
APPLE

An Apple a
Day keeps the
Doctor away

SURAJ PRAKASH

Order this book online at www.trafford.com
or email orders@trafford.com

Most Trafford titles are also available at major online book retailers.

Print information available on the last page.

ISBN: 978-1-4907-9502-7 (sc)
ISBN: 978-1-4907-9501-0 (hc)
ISBN: 978-1-4907-9504-1 (e)

Trafford rev. 05/02/2019

www.trafford.com
North America & international
toll-free: 1 888 232 4444 (USA & Canada)
fax: 812 355 4082

CONTENTS

Preface vii
The Fifth Apple... xiii
Prologue xxi

Winning...1
Background... 5
Life.. 31
Facts on Ground 37
Travel to Shimla 43
Year 2016 67
Space..79
History of Reservation in India 81
Why Jat Agitation 87
A Brief History -
the Introduction of OBC Reservations 113
Forethought 127
An Appeal/Message....................................... 135
Will Cast My Vote 145

Index.. 157
A brief from the author................................. 167

PREFACE

This is a book about true friendship, belief, and togetherness. Standing by in all odds, exploring, and celebrating the winning situations in each other's success. A depiction about exploring the hidden or suppressed energy that forces one to reach out to each other, leave the well-established corporate lives, and plunge into the wide ocean of becoming an entrepreneur and being successful in your own terms.

This book is a faction that touches the hard facts in the reality of life and tries to give an insight to what success is and how it is different for each individual. It tells the journey of each individual through a phase called life and how each individual earns livelihood in best-suited and possible appropriate means. The writer has tried to tell the readers to enjoy the journey along the road, celebrate every success, small or big, as there is no measure of it, and take delight in reaching small destinations instead of looking for the end of the road before enjoyment starts. Live young and live life.

With the current geopolitical situation, which is in critical phase, the book tries to give an understanding as to where the gaps are and what can be plausibly done to bridge those gaps so that we, the citizens of the Republic of India, can see a better and brighter future for the country, for the next generations, and for all of us in the present scenario and thus support the new generation to live a dignified life in the society in the years to come.

The book touches some bitter aspects of society and some tangible angles which are so intriguing that we, being a country with a diverse society and has been dependent for centuries, have come to accept every political decision as a normality. People have been raising their voices and making opinions in an individual capacity or small groups where the need arises to be collective in approach and to start a revolution which will change the future of our nation.

Bharat is a nation that has a century-old history, and no other nation in this world can parallel this. Foreigners have been successful in looting our heritage more than the gold or other valuable reserves, and they have been successful in taking our knowledge reserves to an extent that they have tried their best to destroy our culture and heritage. Today's Bharat, the Republic of India, has stood the test of time, and nothing has been lost. We, the people, have an inborn capability to be recreated from the ashes. So much has been done since pre-independence era to date and much more needs to be aligned and done, and India shall be the superpower of the twenty-first century.

LET MY COUNTRY AWAKE!

Where the mind is without fear
and the head is held high,
where knowledge is free.
Where the world has not been broken up into fragments
by narrow domestic walls. Where words come out from the
depth of truth,
where tireless striving stretches its arms toward perfection.
Where the clear stream of reason has not lost its way
into the dreary desert sand of dead habit.
Where the mind is led forward by thee
into ever widening thought and action.
In to that heaven of freedom, my father,
LET MY COUNTRY AWAKE!"

— Nobel Prize winner Rabindranath Tagore, *Gitanjali*

THE FIFTH APPLE

1. **First Apple**—eaten by Adam and Eve. The start of the whole universe, as it is believed, is through that apple. Adam and Eve ate the **fruit** of knowledge of good and evil in the Garden of Eden, which Adam had been commanded not to do so by God. Adam committed an ancestral sin, and it is a Christian belief that in this state of sin, the fall of man, humanity came into existence, stemming from Adam and Eve's rebellion in Eden—the sin of disobedience in consuming the forbidden fruit from the tree of the knowledge of good and evil. The Garden of Eden is at the head of the Persian Gulf, in southern Mesopotamia, where the Tigris and Euphrates rivers run into the sea and in the Armenian Highlands or Armenian Plateau. Offenses connected to Adam and Eve's act of disobedience were **pride, ambition, and admiration of self.** Man, not satisfied with his own dignity and in the condition he has placed, desire to be equal with God.

Adam believed the devil rather than God and ate the forbidden fruit, and he did not believe that any punishment would overtake him.

Contempt and disobedience to God: This appears in the fact that he ate the fruit contrary to the command of God.

Ingratitude for benefits received: Even though Adam was made in the image of God and for the enjoyment of eternal life, his return for this benefit received was to obey the devil rather than God.

Unnaturalness and the want of love to posterity: Adam did not consider that the gifts God had bestowed upon him and his posterity would be lost not only to himself but also to all his descendants.

Apostasy: By believing and obeying the devil rather than God, Adam wished to obtain equality with God. He set up the devil in the place of God, separating himself from God. Ursinus rightly concludes, "The fall of man was no trifling, nor singular offense; but it was a sin manifold and horrible in its nature, on account of which God justly rejected him, and all of his posterity."

2. **Second Apple**—the one prescribed to keep a healthy body and the sound mind working. As the saying goes, "An apple a day keeps the doctor away." (The proverb was like this: "Eat an apple on going to bed, and you'll keep the doctor from earning his bread.")

Apples have been a recommended fruit and has high nutritious value. Some of the apple's components and their effects on our health are as follows:

Pectin: Pectin is a form of soluble fiber that lowers both blood pressure and glucose levels. It can also lower the levels of low-density lipoprotein (LDL) or bad cholesterol in the body. Pectin, like other forms of fiber, helps maintain the health of the digestive system. Apples are an excellent source of pectin.

Boron: A nutrient found in abundance in apples, boron supports strong bones and a healthy brain. Thus, apple is a very good health supplement.

Quercetin: Reducing allergic responses and boosting immunity, this nutrient shows promise for lowering the risk of various cancers, including cancers in the lungs and breast. It may also reduce free radical damage. Free radicals develop when atoms in the body's cells have unpaired electrons, which can lead to damage to different parts of the cell, including DNA. Quercetin may neutralise free radical damage, which has been implicated in a variety of age-related health problems, including Alzheimer's disease.

Vitamin C: Vitamin C boosts immunity, which helps maintain overall health.

Phytonutrients: Apples are rich in a variety of phytonutrients, including vitamins A and E and beta-carotene. These compounds fight damage from free radicals and can have a profound effect on health, including reducing the risk of heart diseases, diabetes, and asthma.

Apples are rich in iron, and they also act as a toothbrush, cleaning teeth and killing bacteria in the mouth, which may reduce the risk of tooth decay. They're also low in calorie density, one of the trademarks of a healthy food. When a food is low in calorie density, you can eat good-size portions of the food for relatively few calories. In addition, apples are affordable and readily available.

It is the best practice to eat an apple daily and be healthy.

3. **Third Apple**—the apple that fell on Newton's head and which gave rise to modern physics and the theory of gravity, which made flying by air and landing on moon possible.

Isaac Newton changed the way we understand the universe. Revered in his own lifetime, he discovered the laws of gravity and motion and invented calculus. He helped shape our rational worldview. The story of the apple fitted with the idea of an earth-shaped object being attracted to the Earth. It also had a resonance with the Biblical account of the tree of knowledge. The surprising fact is that this tree is still growing at Woolsthorpe Manor today and now must be over 350 years old. Isaac Newton's apple tree is now on its third set of roots but still provides a good crop of apples each summer.

4. **Fourth Apple**—the apple taken away by Apple as its trademark and gave birth to the all-time great magician Steve Jobs.

The very first Apple computer logo, drawn by Ronald Wayne, depicts Isaac Newton under an apple tree. Created by Rob Janoff in 1977, the Apple logo with the rainbow scheme was used from April of that year until August 26, 1999.

Steve Jobs had asserted that the apple logo was inspired by the story of his childhood. The first Apple logo was designed by Steve Jobs and Ronald Wayne in 1976, featuring Isaac Newton sitting under an apple tree. It was a good start, but in the end, Steve wasn't 100 percent convinced, so in 1977, he commissioned designer Rob Janoff to focus more on the apple itself. Janoff said the single bite out of the Apple logo originally served a very practical purpose: scale. The size of the bite showed that the shape was an apple, not a cherry, or any other vaguely round fruit.

> Going to bed at night, saying we've done something wonderful—that's what matters to me.
> —Steve Jobs

5. **I am left lurching in the search of "the fifth apple." I'm sure to find one. Now, the search is ON.**

First book of

Suraj Prakash

To all my family and my friends

When people believe in you, it gives you courage and motivation, but when you believe in yourself, it gives you persistence, determination, and infinite energy. GO!

PROLOGUE

Will the desired results be achieved? Are we doing it right? Is it a good decision? Few of the questions have been crossing the minds of Adi, Manu, and Sunny to the inner core when they took the decision to dump their established careers in the corporate sectors and move on to venture their entrepreneur skills. They believed that Jimmy's decision to join the Defence Services was very good as it gave him a well-protected and secured life as seen and believed by the civilian world. Though all humans are individuals, in the Defence Forces, one has the protected feeling even after being vulnerable to so many difficulties. At this point, there was no return as life is a one-way traffic. Though it's never too late to change and restart to achieve your goals, every passing day keeps increasing life's level of difficulty.

How many people in life work on their personal life goal setting and plan life ahead and in reality strive to achieve that? The 99 percent of those who do so achieve their desired results. The only difficulty is deciding on what a person wants to achieve and setting the goal. In most cases, our goals or goal posts keep changing over time, so as the level of difficulty we want ourselves to be in, as nothing is impossible but nothing is also easy.

Jimmy's career has been on track with its own share of difficulties and struggles. Sunny has always been with a let-go approach and made consistent efforts to achieve the set milestones and the desired goal. Manu has been meticulous and always done in-depth analysis, weighing the pros and cons and outweighing them time and again before he takes the big calculative plunge. Adi accepts the way life goes but has always wanted to be in the list of the richest.

At this stage, failures cannot be accepted, and the worst part of life is fear of failure for the reason that we all know: in India, friends and relatives will laugh at you and keep tormenting on how you did not adhere to the advises given by them from time to time in passing, which were basically to let one feel down more than to uplift the spirit of the so-called entrepreneurs. This is one of the biggest challenges for being in India and in designing your own success story.

WINNING

A goal without a timeline is no goal at all, and to achieve the goal, one must set achievable targets, which should be SMART. Not smart in appearance, but the corporate world has its own elaborative forms as simple, measurable, achievable, result oriented, and time bound. The learning was all done and forgotten in the sector when it comes to actual implementation.

What the intention of leaving the well-established jobs was not made clear, and none has set any so-called SMART goal of life. We all tend to neglect or set aside the most difficult GOAL setting, which is required, be it personal, professional, or financial. The only hindsight was to launch one's own start-up. The big questions are what, where, when, and how.

There were many options which were discussed and evaluated over Skype and conference calls. Adi and Sunny had zeroized on the most optimal one, given their longtime work experience in the Indian market, their understanding of the rationale, and their attachment and affinity to their own native area produce and few big houses that are able to deliver profitable outcomes in the past.

—xxx—

Manu was in India. Adi and Sunny were already at the airport to receive him. It's their first meeting after so many years. Thanks to Facebook, Skype, and WhatsApp which had made it possible to reconnect with the friends who had got busier in their own lives making their own careers post the college days. These new social networks and mobile apps virtually made the world look smaller and rebounded and bonded people's lost connections. It had been more than seven years Manu had met Adi and more than ten years to have met Sunny. All those college days' promises not to part instead live together had fallen apart, and career settlements had taken their priorities.

The eagle had landed, and Sunny and Adi waited eagerly to meet Manu and bash him up. More than ten years had passed since they last met, but the great thing about old friends is that time is not a counter. They meet and greet each other as if they are still as old as when they met the first time. From afar, they could recognise Manu; he was still lean and had maintained his physique, and the corporate sector had enhanced his personality. They maintained their composure and acted as if not recognizing him and letting him approach them first to see if he can recognise Sunny after so many years. Adi had turned his head outside. Manu came straight to Sunny and in a loud voice uttered "Chootiyo!" which means assholes. "Trying your old stunts! You old guys, still not fucking grown-ups." He hurled curses in a voice loud enough and audible to the nearby passengers.

There was a lot of hullabaloo and passers-by could sense that the friends are meeting after a long time. Some smiled, a few cheered by thumbs up, and a few were slightly upset on such a din, but the three were so engrossed in their talks they hardly noticed it, except for Adi, given his nature. It was as if he wanted to finish their talks then and there. Adi moved to get the car, and all were off to the hotel where Manu had booked himself till he gets a place to stay put. Sunny insisted to come along and so did Adi, but Manu preferred the hotel where they can sit and talk with a glass of drink without getting disturbed and catch up on the past ten-plus years.

It was all from life at large and career path to girls, marriage, and family, and finally to their main topic of which all of them have got together for: THE NEW VENTURE'.

Adi started with a brief on the project.

BACKGROUND

Coming Together (2014–2016: New Venture)

When you meet a person, you have met him for life. All it depends is how close you keep the bond going, but the other person cannot be shunted out completely whatever you may do. Spending years together gives a stronger—a bonding which is even closer than the parental and sibling bond and which is called friends. They say destiny is prewritten, and all people in your life come for a reason.

Thirteen years into the corporate world have been an arduous journey, and over the cup of tea, you could hear people discussing their future plans which were mostly inclined towards setting up their own ventures and doing what they intend to do to realise their own true potential. This used to become more prominent after the midterm reviews and more whimsical when annual appraisals were announced. It was always in the news when company made huge percentage profits onshore and offshore, but when it was time to announce the individual incentives, the story had always been turned the other way round. It pushed me to give the over-the-tea discussions a serious thought. Every time an individual gives a serious thought, it gets scary, and time has been the best healer. Mostly, the performance appraisals are announced on Fridays, and you end up in a pub for the good or the bad or whatsoever be the reason. Time flies in muse and abuses any Tom, Dick, or Harry, and by midnight, you actually do not understand which side you are on. Feeling good? Feeling bad? You actually do not know, but it feels better. By Monday, it's the usual another day into the business. This has been the case from year to year.

The capitalist forms of governments and capitalist forms of companies, the so-called MNCs, had only one agenda: to be profitable. That's okay as that's what these companies are here for, but to ensure percentage increase in revenue margin on a year-to-year basis when the company gets tightened because of competition, the companies start to cut cost, and the first thing that comes under the scanner is the employees—the number of employees, employee welfare activities, incentive programmes, trainings, travel, and so on. It starts to demotivate the employees on ground, and no one says a word as everyone has been made aware of the stiff competition outside, be it for the company or the employees.

Personally, the time had come to make the decision. As they say, it's "now or never". The year was 2014.

Four Years: Learning and Yearning, Love Life, Acquaintance, and the End of It

The bell on the door woke him up. It was 3:30 in the hot afternoon. *Who can it be?* He opened the door to find a stranger outside. "Please come in," he offered.

"No, thanks. Here. It's a letter for you." The stranger handed over the letter and turned to leave.

"Thanks!" Sunny murmured, not too audible to the person who had handed him the envelop.

Flipping the envelope back and forth but could not guess the sender, he got back to the crippled bed and wondered who it could be. The handwriting was unpredictable, and there was no name of the writer on the outside of the envelope. *Who can it be, as the hands of all who often write to me are well-distinguished ones anyway.* The letter started.

Sunny! Remember you often without any particular reason. Could not write to you for so long, as I had not heard from you. Met your cousin on the way to Delhi and got to know where you have hidden yourself.

I know you are trying guess who is this. Dear, you will never be able to make out from my handwriting who I am. I have deliberately not mentioned my name anywhere at the beginning or at the end so that you just don't jump to conclusion, and the coming lines will make you acquaint me with a name.

I hope you will be able to recall, but I have not forgotten that you also used to praise my handwriting, and you even tried to copy me. "Sonia, you write so well. Why don't I have that artistic hand?" Ah! It's all bygone for you, but I still don't know what prompted me to write to you.

I know there is nothing much in this letter to share which could have made your reading a pleasure. Sorry for that bit! Still, I am Sonia, if you still have not recalled. At present, I am a teacher at Portmore School Shimla. And by the way, how is Manu, your all-time shy boyfriend.

Hope to hear from you. Bye for now!

It was all a waste of time. *I just call them crazy. I'm never interested in writing letters.* It was all a waste of time, especially when you were off to concentrate on something new and rewarding to work on. Sonia was a sweet girl, and Sunny and Manu both had crush her during their school years, but Sunny was not a person who would hang on. For him, life had to flow, and Manu, not as expressive, would keep things to himself.

"My god, it's 5:20 a.m. now, and I have been in bed for long," he murmured to himself, getting out of the bed. He took a cool shower and put on his new Brazilian outfit. He went outdoors to Cabin 214 on the third floor to catch up with Manu and go for a *gerri* (stroll) drive and dinner anywhere around in town. Sunny was on 6th Floor.

Reaching the door, he found it locked.

Where the hell could Manu be?

There should be no Sundays. It made everyone go lazy, and there was no way to find where Manu could be.

He was still in deep thoughts as he reached the portico where his car was parked. There were hardly any students who had the luxury of a car, but Sunny could afford it for his father was a businessman.

He took out his Esteem car and moved off to the main road without a thought on where he was heading. Reaching the highway crossing, he realised he was directionless, but still, he got down to the one-way road leading to the main city of Bangalore. The campus was just in the outskirts of the sprawling city, and it would soon be part of the main city the way the outskirts were spreading. On the way, he noticed the bright lights of the shopping complexes and hotels. To lighten up his day after a lousy afternoon, he decided to hop into a pub or some cabarets where the live band would be playing as it would be a good start for the evening. He parked his car in the porch of a hotel and moved to the lift. He went to the top floor of the Hotel Royal Orchid, a garden restaurant with a live band. He had heard a lot about its good ambience and food but never got a chance to visit it before. Whenever Manu was with him, he would prefer any small budget hotel or restaurant for two reasons: Manu would insist on it, and he never wanted to hurt his close friend with money show-off.

He had heard that it was a half-covered but also an open restaurant where one could see the city of Bangalore as stars spread on the earth's crest. As he was about to enter the lift, he had to dodge the lady across him; he apologised and got back to give way to the lady. He realised that he was still in the half-awake state, so he pulled his coat sleeves and straightened his gesture. He took a look in the mirror on the front side of the lift, and he could see the lady staring at him. Aside from him and the lady, there was an attendant in the lift who had just greeted them with a pleasant smile. He kept silent against his nature and did not think it right to make any conversation.

Sunny, with a well-built physique and a height of six feet, had good-looking features, and for that matter, he got close looks by females. He could make them feel a connection with him at first sight. He carried an aura where females would like to be in his company and love to chat with him. His eyes were good enough to do the talking which he never failed to use. It took a while for the lift to reach the top floor, and nobody broke the silence.

The moment he stepped into the restaurant, he could feel the air of discomfort with the attendant. "Sir, may I know your reservation details."

"No, I haven't made any."

"Sorry, sir. We are extremely sorry, but we don't have any tables vacant as all tables are booked for today."

Sunny did not realise that the restaurant might be so much in demand and that one needed to have a booking for the evening especially on the weekends. The weekend culture had creeped in this technologically growing city, which had more of the software students and youth working in the technology hubs.

"No problems at all, I did not realise there would so much of a rush."

"It's okay."

As he turned to leave, the lady in the elevator was in front of him, and before he could step aside, she spoke, "Would you mind joining me? I have the bookings."

It was so instantaneous that he could not think it through and just moved along with her to the designated table. Both made themselves comfortable on the chairs, but none spoke a word. There was light music in the background and pleasant lights on the center of the table; there was still more time left for the live band to take the stage.

Finally, Sunny broke the silence. "Hi, I am Sunny, final year student at RVCE Bangalore. Though I belong to Shimla, I am here for studies. How about you?"

"Officially, I am Neol, but you can call me Neelu."

"You belong to Bangalore?" Sunny shot back out of habit.

"No, I am from Pune."

"Oh! Then, how come such a name?"

Sunny had the nature of being blunt in asking, although it was little inappropriate in this first meeting and even before knowing each other.

"I like them both. Whenever I go home, I am Neelu. When I'm here, I am Neol."

"Are you on a job over here?"

"Not exactly. I am on a job. I am married but . . . " She gave a long pause and did not speak for a while, leaving the sentence unfinished.

"It's okay. I think it's something you should keep to yourselves. No worries."

The big drum of jazz made them look towards the stage. The drummers were testing their instruments in the mild tone.

Sunny, through his eyes, made a request for the attendant, and the next moment, he was there.

"What would you care to have today, sir?"

He ushered him towards the lady.

"Sure!" "For me, Long Island iced tea."

"Anything else, ma'am?"

"No. Later."

"For me, Sazerac Cognac," Sunny adds.

They had long chat on random topics.

Neelu was a beautiful lady in her mid-twenties. From her outfit and looks, it was difficult to judge if she was a student or married. In just an hour or so, the two had gotten so aquatinted as if they knew each other for years.

By the time Sunny realised the time, it was already a quarter past twelve. The very next moment, he excused himself to leave and without much delay left the place in a hurry.

The expression on Neelu's face changed suddenly as if someone poured a bucket of ice-cold water on her. She could not say no nor ask him to stay a bit longer, so she uttered, "Okay, bye. See you."

Without any delay, Sunny was off. Neelu wanted to have his contact, but before she could ask, it was too late. He was already gone. She kept sitting and thinking of the past three or four hours she had spent with him and of the talks she had shared with him. The cabaret had closed long back, but the restaurant was still on the go with the customers. Neol asked the waiter for the cheque. She settled the bill and just thought to herself, could it be that he just escaped payout of the cheque? The next moment, she shrugged it off.

She thought of how she had seen him driving in a luxury car, and from what he had told her about himself, it seemed he came from a very good background, and his dressing sense had that persona. He must have missed and now remembered some urgent work but so late in the middle of the night.

She left the table still engrossed in her thoughts about Sunny.

It was nearing one when Sunny arrived back at the hostel and realised that Manu's cabin lights were still on. He thought to pay him a visit, kick his ass first, narrate him the Sunday's happenings, and if time permits catch up on some books. It was the final semester; otherwise he never bothered studying. As exams were around the corner, he thought to spend some time with books, which he never liked. He had been able to manage his grades somehow for past four years, but this time, it seemed tougher.

Upon reaching Cabin 214, he found the door shut. As he tried to knock, the door opened a little. He pushed the door and got inside only to find Manu in deep slumber. He tried to shake him up, but he realised Manu was drunk, and he knew of his habit that after drinks, it was not possible to wake him up.

He straightened his cover, removed the old novel half-crushed under his head, closed the dripping from the tap, switched off the lights, and left for his room.

As he opened the door to his room, he found it quiet and deserted; he felt lonely but also wanting to sleep. He changed his attire and switched on the table lamp to sit down and study. The meeting with Neol was still fresh in his mind; on the other hand, exams were making him a bit restless. He tried to go through the first page but could not cope up for more than fifteen minutes, and minutes later, he was fast asleep.

—xxx—

The bright sunshine woke Manu up. He realised he was a bit later than usual and also had a headache from the previous night's hangover. He went to shower and stayed there for some time to get sober, then he dressed up and left his room to join Sunny.

However, Sunny's cabin was locked. He knew Sunny had early classes, and that might be the reason. He laughed to himself thinking about Sunny's concern towards studies at the last hour. Is it just showbiz, or had he turned serious towards it? Whatever!

As he was about to enter the dining area, he saw Sunny in front of another hostel, talking and laughing with one of the girls whose face was not known. But that doesn't matter; for Manu, all female's faces were unknown, and for Sunny, all faces were familiar, and even if he did not know, it did not take him time to get introduced and know them. The very next moment, Sunny drove off with the girl he was talking to in his car. Manu smiled to himself and left for breakfast as he was getting late.

Sunny and Manu had been friends since childhood. They had been boarders in school and had always been together. One was the north pole, and the other was south, but what made them stay together was never understanding—it was just love and a no-hate friendship. Their views were alike to an extent, but when it came to females, Sunny always loved to be in their company, whereas Manu was reserved and took too long to open up. But this never bothered any of them. They never had any contradictions, and even though they were from a different school of thought, they had developed an understanding that with ease they were able to find midway whenever there was conflict. Sunny came from a well-to-do business background, whereas Manu was from a nice family. They still stayed together and never had any differences even for money matters. Sunny was lavish and spendthrift to an extent, whereas Manu was conservative. Most of the time, however, it was Sunny who ran out of cash and sought help from Manu for his girls' nights out. Manu would love to find a solitary place for a drink in the evening, which should not be expensive at all.

Since they had been together since school days, nothing was hidden from each other; they had been together through thick and thin and would seek each other's advice on all practical or impractical matters. For Manu, Sunny's stories with girls were very fascinating, and the way Sunny would narrate them with all the more spice, Manu would sometimes feel pity for those girls but was sure they also had good fun on Sunny's expense. There are some times he even scolded him for always spending so much money on girls, and Sunny would promise not to do it next time, but whenever he meets a new face, he forgets Manu's warnings and goes back to his usual self.

Adi was the only one from the north who became their friend in college. He was closer to Manu than Sunny, but he understood Sunny well for his nature. Adi was from Chandigarh, and being from the north studying in the south town of India was one of the factors that brought them together. Adi would play a balancing act whenever there was utter conflict or difference of opinion; he would play the trump card in decision-making and drawing the conclusions.

Adi would accompany Sunny only when Manu was along as he knew that only Manu could handle Sunny in times when he was off the grid.

Manu met Sunny that evening, and Sunny had narrated to him all that happened from Sunday afternoon onwards, starting it form the letter from Sonia.

"You remember Sonia?" he asked.

"Yes, I do!"

"O-ho. You remember her. I thought you were never interested."

Manu gave a candid look at Sunny. "Remembering and being interested are two different things, my boy."

"Okay. Don't take it to heart. She had written me a letter after so many years, *yaar*. She still remembers how I used to admire her handwriting."

"Nothing new. You used to admire all girls for some reason or the other."

"That's what I mean, man. She has taken that compliment seriously and remembers it till now. She is a teacher in Portmore School at Shimla. But I'll tell you one thing, bro. You were also eyeing her. Our difference is you never told her, but she did mention to me about you." Sunny wanted to tease Manu.

"And then, you never told me."

"If I had told you, I would have lost her."

"You scoundrel! You have had so many girlfriends, and one was trying to approach me, but you did not have the curtsy to inform me. Fuck you, man."

"This was the first time Sunny had seen Manu getting perturbed on the mention of the girl. He was happy for him but also wanted to tease him for keeping his feelings hidden.

Manu had decided to meet Sonia whenever he visited Shimla back on holidays. It had been more than four years; he had been out of town, and whenever he got some time during breaks at college, they would visit some or other places and hardly stayed in Shimla. Manu had been having a secret crush on Sonia, and on a few odd times, he met her during school years but never got the chance or had the opportunity to mention it to her. Had it been Sunny, he would have announced it on top of his voice and made it known to all.

For Manu, it was different.

Exams were over, and both of them, Sunny and Manu, had planned to go via Bombay. Sunny would stay put with his father for some time, and Manu would leave back for Shimla and start to look for job interviews. He already had a few during his last month in the campus, but nothing had come out yet. Sunny had made the train reservations to avoid last minute hassles. They had decided to travel by train to enjoy the journey en route. The car would come through. Adi would be leaving early through a direct route to attend to his family function.

Everyone was busy taking leave from their old and new friends. They were not sure when they shall all meet together after this. It was their last night, and before leaving, they decided to go for a big celebration.

Adi wanted his own time to see off Suchitra, a local of Bangalore and his classmate, and Manu had no hassles being alone, so he had packed up and got ready to move.

On the other hand, before the evening, Sunny had already decided that they should celebrate in the garden restaurant of Hotel Royal Orchid in the heart of the city. He made the table bookings in advance this time. For Manu, all restaurants were equally good as long they can serve booze at the cheapest price possible.

It was 5:30 p.m., and Sunny had reached Manu's cabin. Manu was in the shower, so he started to look for some old magazines, but they were all worn out. He took out the cassette from the rack and placed it in the small stereo beside Manu's bedside table. As he pushed the button, he could hear the yell from the bathroom.

"Hey! Who is this?"

"It's me, boy," Sunny replied in a calm tone.

"Manu peeped out of the door, fully naked and with soap dripping on his body. "Hey, you are ready, but isn't it too early, man?"

"Come on, make it fast. You know there is a reservation required to be seated."

"No worries. We can find some other place. There is no death of restaurants in the city of Bangalore."

"You first get in and make it fast. We will discuss on the way."

"Okay, okay!"

Sunny again started to scuffle the books and found a diary under some old books. The diary was two years old. He flipped through the pages and found that it was quite filled. He glanced through the pages and found a reference of the name Sonia at many a place. The bathroom door unbolted, so he placed the diary back where it was.

"Why are we in so much hurry and dressed so early? You mentioned that live music starts past eight," Manu asked.

"*Yaar*, there is a problem of reservation of tables, and on the weekends, there's a hell of a rush."

"Then why don't you reserve one on the phone?"

"That's a good idea. I will go for it, and you must be ready by that time." Sunny had already done the reservation but was in no mood for elaborated discussion.

"Okay. I will be there in ten minutes."

"Ten means ten!"

Sunny left the place, and by the time he took a stroll and was back, he saw Manu was ready and standing in front of a mirror, giving a touch up to his dress and as usual, smoking his Marlboro. Sunny came close, took off his cigarette, and asked him to get ready faster.

He knew Sunny's habit of just making things look much important, which were of no interest to Manu. Both left the place in their best attires for the evening celebrations, and it took close to half an hour to reach the place.

They reached the top and found their table booked well in front of the door, with an overview of the glass window. One could view the full hall very easily. Both made themselves comfortable. It was just fifteen past six and too early for Manu.

The attendant came to the table and placed the menu cards in front of both of them. Without a glance, Manu asked for a light lager beer and looked towards Sunny for his order, who he found preoccupied somewhere else.

"Hey, where are you?" Manu inquired.

"I will just not take anything yet."

"Why? You made us come so early to this place."

"I just like that. You go ahead."

Manu asked for the lager and some cheese dips. The attendant left the table.

He observed Sunny looking a bit perplexed and uneasy.

"Young man, what's bothering you? Any problems?"

Sunny could no longer conceal the real purpose of his coming here.

"It was Neol, or Neelu, to be precise. I met her two weeks back on Sunday evening, and we shared the table as I did not have any reservations like I told you."

Manu laughed to himself. He told Sunny, "I bet I could guess it from the moment you were in my cabin so early to go out that something is not right."

"Don't worry. Wait for some time, she will come," Sunny replied.

"She will come, my heart says."

"Oh, so nowadays, your heart has also started saying something about females. You better concentrate on your booze and just neglect it if I get the chance for some kissing and wishing."

"By god, you are a crazy junk."

They were into all these discussions when Manu could notice a broad smile on Sunny's face, and his gaze was fixed on the doorway. Manu also looked towards the door and noticed a beautiful blonde standing at the reception.

Sunny waved his hand, looking much delighted, and the next moment, the female at the counter started to walk towards their table.

The exchanged cheerful greetings, and Sunny introduced Manu to Neol (Neelu).

Both exchanged hellos, and Neelu made herself comfortable beside Sunny on the sofa.

"How are you?" Sunny asked Neelu.

"I am fine and a bit confused. You left that day so suddenly that I thought we wouldn't get to meet again. It's good that you came," Neelu replied.

"I was in a hurry and forgot to give you my contact, but you knew my college. I don't have a phone to contact you, but I forgot to ask yours."

Both got busy in their discussions, and Manu kept sipping his beer and studying the lady's face and features. He had no interest in them, but he was a good psychologist even without taking any formal course or training. He could make out that she was a broad minded female and would not mind to mingle with unknown faces. It did not take long for her to get acquainted with any stranger, and she was more of a Sunny-type in nature. The problem with two people similar in nature is that when they get together, initially, they will feel joyous, but soon, egoism creeps in.

She must be around twenty-six or seven but looked younger and had a personality to easily impress others. She had a very sweet voice and on top of that a very polite way of complaining, which girls usually have when they are in a new friendship or relationship. She gained the affirmative thoughts of Manu. He could definitely judge to an extent that she was looking for a trusted male protection and support.

He was busy in his thoughts while Sunny and Neol were busy chatting. He then felt something on the contrary. On the front sofa, there was only Neol, and Sunny was missing. Neol was staring at him. He first shook himself, and without a second thought, he asked Neol as to where Sunny had gone?

"Don't you know? He told you before he left that he would make a call to Bombay."

"Oh!"

Neol's mind was racing as she was drawing the comparison between Sunny and Manu. Both were so close friends. Manu was not as charming as Sunny but had a chiseled face and a built-up physique. His face had expressions of contentment, and his eyes were impressively sharp.

Manu disturbed her thoughts when he asked, "What would you care to have?"

"No thanks. Nothing yet."

To break the ice, Manu started to ask about her and how she came in acquaintance with Sunny. He asked so many other questions here and there, and he could make out that Neol was married and presently either not in good terms with her husband or already divorced. For the first time, he felt some uneasiness in her presence. He felt an unsaid liking, and not being able to understand the reason, he wanted to get closer to her and hug her tightly. He shrugged himself on the thought; on the other hand, he knew that for Sunny, females are a pastime, and he does not get attached for a long time. Maybe that was the reason Manu was having these unsaid feelings.

He could see Sunny enter the doorway, so he left the table himself and went to the bar counter and got himself a drink.

"What would you take, Sunny?" Manu asked when he got back to them, but Sunny confirmed he had placed the order for himself and Neol.

"Okay, my boy!" Manu had a bit of tone in his voice for no apparent reason.

It was a great evening and already 1:00 a.m. when all three came out from the restaurant. It was a bit chilly outside.

Sunny offered Neol to come with them as it was quite late for her to return back through the bizarre roads at night. First, she kept quiet, but on the condition that she will leave early morning, she agreed to come along.

Sunny handed over the car keys to Manu, and he took the rear seat with Neol. The car was just on the dark road, and Manu was concentrating on his driving, although there were hardly any few odd vehicles were on the road. Everyone was silent, but Sunny, as usual, had something else racing in his mind. He slipped his hand on her thighs, and she didn't move or even look towards him but kept silent. He kept caressing her, and she did not show any reaction, so he planted a kiss on her neck. She shivered on her seat and moved away. She felt the presence of Manu and hesitated a bit, but she kept quiet lest Manu would find out what they were doing. But Sunny was unstoppable and was not crossing the limits. It had been close to year since she got separated from his husband, but her heart still could not allow her this way. Sunny again slipped his hand underneath, and this time, she retaliated loudly and pushed him away.

"Please behave yourself. I want to go back to my place. If this was your intention, it would have been better not to come along to accompany you."

"Manu," she continued, "please drop me back at the hotel. I will go back by a taxi." By this time, they had already entered the gates of the hostel.

Manu stopped the car for Sunny to comment, but Sunny got down and asked Manu to go and drop her at her place.

Manu did not say a word. He started the engine and drove off. He could see Sunny moving out to his cabin a bit in despair, through the rearview mirror.

It did not take much time for them to reach Neelu's place. Except for the directions, they did not speak any other word.

Neelu got down and came over to the driver's side window as he put the ignition off.

"Forget what happened. This is the first time you have come. Please come on in." She sounded quite normal.

Manu closed the car ignition and followed her. He did not say anything on what had happened since Sunny was his heart-loving friend, and for Manu, Sunny was never wrong and whatever he did, girls were equally responsible.

"Why did you agree to accompany him at this hour of night if you did not have any thought of this kind?"

"I did not know his main purpose of friendship was something else," she replied, her tone a bit pinching. Manu did not say anything further. She opened the door and switched the lights on. It was a big place, very well decorated and the furniture elegantly placed with big hangings on the walls. Manu made himself comfortable on the nearest available chair. Neelu went inside and got him a glass of beer.

"I think I have had enough and have to drive back," he said.

"Have a sip. It's not much."

He took a few quick gulps, placed the glass back on the table corner, and stood up to leave.

Neelu came near him, and with very polite words, she murmured, "Sorry, Manu. I am very sorry for what happened."

"It's all right."

She started to sob.

Manu did not know what to do, so he took her in his arms and smothered her back.

In his big arms and chest, Neelu felt a sense of protection as if nobody on this earth can harm her at this instance. Both kept standing in the same position for a long time. Then she took out her face and looked deep into Manu's eyes. Her expressions were inviting. She raised herself on her toes and kissed Manu's lips with a long, hot smooch. Manu could feel her tongue in his mouth. He lifted her in his arms and placed her gently on the sofa and laid his half-weight on her. She quivered and grabbed him as if trying to save herself from fear of drowning in the deep waters.

It was all so instant, and Manu could feel her famine fragrance. It was very pleasant and exciting. His hands started to slip all over her silky body and separating each layer of clothes she had worn. Moments later, both were stark naked under the bright lights, and Neelu had such a curvy body that Manu could not control himself.

He drove back home, and when he reached the hostel gates, it was almost close to four in the morning. He parked the car and saw that Sunny's room lights were still on. He straightaway went over to his room, the door was open, and Sunny was sitting with his legs crossed and placed on the table, with fag in his hand.

Manu came and snatched away the cigarette, "It's not good. You don't smoke, so better refrain." This annoyed Sunny, but he knew of his own habit, so he kept quiet. It was very depressing for him to take a no from a female, and up to date, he had never failed in his attempts.

Manu sat on the chair alongside him and tickled on his ear.

"So how was your trip back to her home? Did she say anything later?"

"No, but she felt sorry to have behaved like this with you. She was expecting something else, but you took her like your other female friends."

"Fuck it, *yaar*."

"That's not the only way you can deal with all females you come across. I have been warning you for the same thing many a times."

"Manu, you know I am not interested in lectures and especially at this hour of time, and if you are so keen and interested, I will try fix up your marriage with her."

Manu felt it wrong, but guessing the situation, he changed the topic. "Leave all that. It's quite late, and let's go to sleep and get up on time to catch the train or we might miss it." Sunny did not say a word, so Manu wished him a good night and left for his cabin.

Sunny could still not gather his thoughts, and although he went off to bed, he remained awake just thinking of Neelu. He felt a bit of pang internally. Engulfed in his thoughts, he did not come to know when he was off to sleep.

Adi came in the early morning and woken them up as he was leaving via a different rout and train. He left with a promise to catch up on them while in Chandigarh.

Both reached the station well in time for the train. Though there was a lot of rush, both were silent to themselves. The rush and din did not bother them, for they had their reservations in place. From their late night yester to their early morning awakening and leaving the college, all the events had left them with mixed feelings. They reached their coach, looked for their names in the chart, and went to settle at their respective seats. Placing their bags in place, Manu asked Sunny if he wants a cup of coffee.

"No, I would not like to go out. I am fine here and am tired. There were still more than twenty minutes for departure."

He stood on the door for a moment and took a view of the public on the platform. There was a lot of hustle and bustle going on, but suddenly, he jolted as he saw Neelu at the far end approaching their coach. He could not think what to do: go to her or just come back inside and wait for her. He kept standing there in ignorance till Neelu came and touched him on his arm; He acted to have been taken by surprise and not expecting her there at all.

"Hi, how are you?" she greeted.

"Hello! How come you came to know we are here?"

"Sunny had mentioned it yesterday."

"Oh!"

"Where is he?"

"He is inside. Come on in."

Both approached the cubicle where Sunny was busy reading a novel.

"Hey, Sunny!"

"Hello," Sunny replied in a weak tone.

"I think you are still annoyed."

"What right do I have to get annoyed at you? I am sorry for whatever happened."

"It's all right if you need to feel so. How long you are going to be off?"

"Don't know. Right now, no next plan yet."

The train had sounded its first whistle, and it could run any time.

"I will wait for you," she said, and she started to sob. Both Sunny and Manu sat in perplexity not knowing what they should do.

Manu eyed Sunny to make her quiet and left the place himself.

In a moment, the train jolted to start and crawl slowly. Neelu got on her feet, planted a kiss on Sunny's lips, and left. She came out and rushed for the door and went off. Manu saw that she was quiet but looking grim, and she did not even look at him or wish him goodbye.

Somewhere in the depth of his heart he felt the pain of feeling neglected. He came back to the cubicle, and the train had already caught pace. He noticed Sunny was quite in a light mood now.

"Hey, what took you so long?" Sunny asked.

"Nothing—just standing at the doorway. What did she say?"

"Nothing special, just made a promise that in the earliest possible, I must come and meet her and that she will wait for me."

"So what's your plan? Going along or dropping off at the next station?"

"Ha-ha," Sunny just laughed it off.

It was a long but a joyous journey, and as the train was approaching Bombay, Sunny had packed up his baggage. Manu was to travel further, so he was just thinking of the days ahead without Sunny. He wished Adi could have also come along so this route and the remaining journey could have been exciting, but Adi had his family commitment that he had to reach early.

At the station, both parted and Sunny wished Manu good luck for the time ahead and with a promise to meet him soon. Sunny did not have any plans to visit Shimla this time as he would try and assist his father in the business. Though he always thought to be independent and set up his own venture, he required money, and he had to earn it as his father, being a strict financer, would not just pass him the bucks to experiment with it. Manu left the train with a promise of the earliest possible drop by at Sunny's and that with Adi, all three of them would catch up in Chandigarh.

Sunny joined hands with his father to support his business house. Engineering has not been very useful directly, but otherwise, he could be logical in his approach. Sunny got to handle the accounting department, and it was a Herculean task for him as he had to be in the office on time to work with the team till late evenings and update his boss—his dad—each day on the overall company expenses and profitability.

Sunny, who had lived his life as a vagabond, had gotten trapped to follow timelines, conduct himself soberly, and be dedicated to the business interests. The lady killer has been tamed. He did not have any friends in the city and missed Manu a lot. He called up Manu whenever he felt lonely, but the business in the company left hardly any free time.

The only free time he had was early mornings till the start of office hours where he would go for his morning gym which hardly left any time to idle, as well as on Sunday afternoons when he would be free from all chores, but he hated this time as well. He would usually drive on the roads of Bombay and sometimes on Marine drive all the way to Worli Sea Phase and be back late at night to have dinner at home. This was the time he missed Manu a lot and remembered the time from collage.

Manu had his first appointment in the telecom sector in Calcutta, and because of the growing sector, it hardly left any time for Manu to get back and touch base with Sunny or Adi.

Adi had made it to a software and networking company, looking after the government sector's new LAN and WAN networks or expansions. It was a monotonous work, but there were hardly any other better options in the small city of Chandigarh. The only sector which was a buzz was telecommunication.

—xxx—

LIFE

The pleasant weather was so welcoming that you would fall in love with the place. It was not too hot and nor too cold, and there were warm winters and cool summers. You can swim and bask in the sun any time of the year. Each day has been a pleasure as work pressures had been complimented with work-life balance, and it was fun to be with new people in a new country.

It had been a sudden decision to shift from the well-established career in the Indian Telecom Industry. Manu one day decided to quit and take up the opportunity abroad. It posed a different kind of challenge and uncertainty, but Manu had made up his mind to shift the gear and see the world from a different angle.

In the beginning, the schedule to get settled in an entire new world and faces had been challenging, but with time, it had become so homely and the people so friendly. The weather was loving and temperatures were awesome year around. It had been a good career move, which had position, career growth opportunity, and of course, well payoff and benefits taken care by the MNC. The long pending dream of Manu had finally been realised to an extent, which was to visit foreign land and in particular, to roam the world.

The first few months had been hectic. He was Setting things up and getting on to align his work which was more or less similar to what Manu was doing in India. for the technological requirements, the fast-changing world had to bring up the network to a level of a new and changed management, and he had to meet and exceed their expectations. How the year slipped by, Manu could hardly believe himself. His work was normally a routinely matter apart from a few critical annual operations and business plan meetings and other financial alignments.

Manu thought it was the right time to take a time off as it had been long since he joined the place, and he had been continuously busy as there was a total change in his work setup. Being near perfectionist, it had been a daunting task to scale up the network and shift to the new setup of managing and operating the network" through his third company. There was an entire manpower shift to his new work and culture, which had its own teething problem to be resolved and aligned.

Two years had just flown away. Though there was a lot of learning and humungous work pressures in keeping with the completion of work timelines and customer satisfaction, the scores were depleting even with consistent efforts. It seemed to be not in the right direction, or the team has not been able to judge the market. The main basic reason was the customer on ground loosing trust. Why? There were intermingled issues, and it was too hard steering the changes by the top management. The initial start was smooth, but there was a cultural shock when the entire pace was jolted by the new communication change, and then it started to create a turmoil.

Zambia, or for that matter the whole African continent, got independent forty years hence, but internally, they were still dependent, which meant that most of the business houses were still controlled by the British and French. The workforce was unionised, and the leaders of those unions exploited the manpower and made money on their behest.

For any concerns faced by the employees, the union would come in and act as mediator for negotiations, which would then reach a mutual agreement from both the employee and employer. At times, this was a controversial area wherein the union had a political setup and a say in the government, which would then lead to unwanted pressure.

All the material, equipment, clothes, medicine, and even daily necessities were still imported from European or Asian countries. The cost of living was still very high, and the rich were becoming richer and more powerful, whereas the poor remain in poverty. There was no end to it. The wildlife tourism and copper export, being major sources of economic growth houses, are majorly owned through FDI.

The Corporate (2010–2013 Corporate Abroad, Entrepreneur Decision, and Working)

A sudden meeting was called, and all the directors were to be in the boardroom in the next fifteen minutes. All were in their offices only, as it was a Monday and the first day of the month.

On the way to the boardroom, there was an empty alleyway, and it seemed everyone was too preoccupied with after-weekend works. The first person to arrive at the boardroom was the EA, and then later the managing director (MD), who was as frivolously dressed as ever. With a cheerful and skirmish smile, she welcomed Manu with a "Good morning, dear. All are waiting for you." She had been continuously calling his cell phone, and from her greetings, it was more than obvious that things were not in line. *Oops! That means I am the last one to arrive.*

The problem to being the last person to arrive was getting seated to the nearest line of fire. It was surprising to find the CEO International across the table, and it was an indication that something was drastically wrong. His early morning presence in the boardroom was not a good sign.

Taking the only seat left with no other option, everyone waited in silence to see Manu settle in. The task was completed in few seconds, and all eyes shifted questionably to the boss-CEO sitting at the tail end of the table.

"Good morning, everyone." The CEO broke the silence with a greeting, which was too reserved to be reverted. The usual enthusiastic revert was missing in everyone's tone as they all wanted to show seriousness to the occasion while eagerly waiting for the news or discussion.

"Gentlemen, I was with the management team in Nairobi yesterday, and a few changes in the management have been discussed and agreed and shall be implemented with an immediate effect. These are being done to align with the future course of action keeping in view the company and personnel growth and of course, alignment to the competitor's market strategy.

"Under this, the decision has been made that your MD shall be moving to international assignment wherein he shall form part of the advisory board. A new group has been formulated which will be headed by him and a small team from all functions will be made to join him, and they shall be responsible for new technology projects and evaluate the short-term and long-term impact on the company's growth and presence in the region. His main role will be to advise the board on the requirements by taking the global inputs across countries and technologies and after completing evaluations, present the case for implementation in marked countries.

"This shall help us position ourselves in the region as an innovative company, which is inclined and committed to enhance technological growth and thus contribute to overall economic growth. The change will be effective from tomorrow, and until we are able to bring in another MD, the COO will act as an MD. Your present MD is available locally for the time being and will be able to help out any information on the handover.

"Gentlemen, if you have any questions or discussions, you are free to air them." Some of them were sitting with their jaws dropped while listening to the CEO, and none of them could understand the reason for such a sudden change. Manu was personally unsure whether to celebrate the occasion of the MD's promotion to the international management ring or to feel sad of such a sudden departure. But one thing was for sure, something was amiss, although it was not obviously visible as of now.

—xxx—

FACTS ON GROUND

All the background works were done. The job looked so simple, but it had its own complexities as it required thinking beyond how a common man practically shaped things on ground. The basics of company formation and registrations were completed, and all the required infrastructure for the project was put in place. Financial costs were the main concern because of the limited resources available at hand, and the aim to avoid overspending enthusiastically was well held up.

Sunny had now become good financial manager and same, was being handled by him. He had the capability to execute meticulously, and that was the reason for him to hold the financial spends. His changed style of becoming serious in the execution of any work was a sea change in his persona. Working with his father, he had acquired the accounts management skills inherently.

During the first visit of acquisition, Adi and Manu also accompanied Sunny to the locations, and with the pre-connections on the ground, they met the local dealers over there. Long hours of meetings were done. All three realised that they do not belong to the world they were going to venture in, and working there was entirely different to what they have managed during their corporate years of customer engagements. Their clients from the corporate world were dressed in formal attires and ties. There would be pre-mail meeting requests sent to everyone concerned, containing the agenda of the meeting, points to be discussed, and copies would be sent to all concerned bosses. The minutes of meeting (MOM) should be prepared and circulated to everyone in the responsibility matrix, along with closure timelines.

Here, there was no such thing. Few sellers dressed in local attires came in for discussion and were little surprised the way this was being done as they have also not done any organised meetings, and the only meetings they attended were related to Panchayat elections or the like.

Being new to business norms, all three were interested to pick up knowledge to whatever extent possible from the locals. Their basic aim and agenda was to align the good product produce procurement and know how it was distinguished on the ground. There was a fair good flow of knowledge from the young and old locals, and there were words of expertise from the agents and the elderly, The three were all ears to every word they said lest they miss some important information, which shall come handy in the due course of time.

Visits were made to the countryside orchards, and different varieties of apples were shown by one of the elderly persons whose name was Mr. Hukam Singh. He had been in to the apple growing business for the past fifty years and more, and he had seen the very good and bad times of produce. Mr. Hukam was also very knowledgeable of all products as he had lived his life in and out over there.

The selling of apples had been done since ages, when a middleman would come and put the price to the orchard even before the produce is ripe. A token amount would be paid up then and there, which would be a maximum of 5-7 percent of the expected produce value. The produce would then be picked up when ripe and get sold in the market, and payments would be made through cheques which had their own payment timelines of a few months later. The producers were not happy as the cheque would take time to materialise, and they were at the mercy of the buyer. There would even be some times when it would not get cashed out because of insufficient funds in the buyers' accounts.

All those who came to join the meeting were feeling happy as they were promised on-the-spot payment as per the market rate evaluation and quality and quantity of produce. They were eager to do business with the three, and word of mouth had spread across the region over mobile conversations; as it seemed, they all knew each other closely.

Mr. Hukam was also kind enough to offer them homemade lunch which was prepared in Desi ghee (clarified butter), which they were not used to, being too health conscious. Having no option, they accepted the invitation, and all the members of the family made all-out efforts to ensure their visitor would have the best experience of hospitality. New plates and spoon sets were opened, and a new cloth spread on the table was placed. After all the good talks on fresh air, pleasant weather, and the lovable people, the conversation turned back to apples. It was indeed a different experience for Adi, Sunny, and Manu.

By the time the evening dawned, all were tired and looking forward to a much-needed break. Their enthusiasm of the morning had gone down a bit because of tiredness, but none of them would admit it as their spirits were internally high and their commitment to work was of utmost importance.

It was nine by the time they all returned and arrived back at the hotel which was not too far from their previous location. Before even getting freshened up, Manu had ordered a drink to his room, and by the time Sunny and Adi got freshened up as well, his drink had arrived. Adi and Sunny smiled it off as they knew Manu would not wait for them, and so they placed their own orders for food and drinks.

They had a long flow of discussion from all ends, regarding the experiences they gained and trying to interpret what the locals actually meant and what they could take out from their discussions with them. They figured out what would be the cautions, which shall need to be taken in this new form of business method, and what would be the reactions of the bigger giants in the market, as well as how all the holes would be plugged and how they can move forward.

The morning brought a feeling of fresh air and a rejuvenating start. By the time of breakfast, they were all packed up and set to move back to Chandigarh.

Sunny asserted that from the next time on, only one of them should visit the locations at a given time. As he was back on financials, he confirmed that the cost incurred during their trip and their stay was quite heavy on their pockets, and with this, the company cannot have cash flows for sustainable business. To an extent, it was agreed by everyone that since this was their first visit, all of them were required to attend.

Slowly but steadily, some inroads have been made into the setup of the new business house and work, and it had started to move in the right direction. There was a hell lot of running around, and taking the smallest inputs to their strides, a headway was made, and the local and urban combination of business functioning was rolled out.

Money exchange had started in and out of banks, and Sunny had been keeping close monitoring and tracking of all the inward and outward payments and would keep giving highlight on almost a daily basis as to the financial status of the business. They were all moving forward, and everything looked positive and promising in the long run.

—xxx—

TRAVEL TO SHIMLA

(2004: Meeting a New Love)

Discover, has already has a past with Sam. Sam came back from abroad. Manu moved on to another corporate house for better opportunity and to get away from the feeling of losing the love.

On this trip, Manu had to travel alone as it was discussed and decided to reduce the expenses being incurred in this new launched venture. Traveling alone was a bit boring and had no fun other than listening to the songs or making a few calls here and there on the way. Manu was preoccupied in his thoughts and started to compare the current situation to the ones he had during his corporate days.

When he was traveling for a corporate trip, he was full of energy, but he was so much preoccupied with work that there was no time for leisure or viewing the scenic sights. Sitting on the back seat, he was engaged in refining the data, aligning the power point presentations, scanning the bombarding questions from the management, and looking for possible reasonable answers or the escape routes.

The journey through the snake route was nostalgic and taking him back down the memory lane. The best part in corporate works, which Manu enjoyed the most, was team building sessions which he looked forward to eagerly every year. This was from the early years of his start in corporate life, and three years into it, Manu thought to himself that those were the best of times. There was a lot of travelling for work, but every day had new challenges, and that was what he enjoyed the most.

The telecommunications industry had started to boom, and all service providers and operators were expanding their network coverage. Calling costs were coming down, and people had started to accept mobile technology, and the future with data was at the back end, while voice calls were the priority. There were lots of movements happening, and this created a buzz and positivity in the market. Spending twelve to even fourteen hours in the office had become a normal routine, but Manu was getting a good career growth, so all was good, and other than that, there was a very good culture in the company, and the equally good number of females around made all the more sense to be at work than be back to a the boring guesthouse.

Companies had good earnings and margins, and they were very liberal in spending for their employees' welfare. Since the MNC had a European culture, flat hierarchy, open approach, it enabled employees to work to effortlessly deliver their best.

Any new contract, which was bagged by the company, was celebrated with bottles of champagne, and with the small number of the team, almost everyone had a bottle to splurge towards the end of the office hours. Small or big, all wins were celebrated with lots of fun, and welcoming the start of a new work or a teamwork was acknowledged, and the associated team would be appreciated by the top management.

There were TGIFs (thank God it's Friday). The good things about MNCs was that they work officially for five days, and hence Friday evenings were the most welcoming time. After a long week, weekends were eagerly awaited, and Friday was considered a lovely weekday. The day would start winding towards five in the evening and will end up late at night in the clubs or pubs.

Manu thought to himself how lovely those times were in the company of friends and girlfriends. All his friends were always poking him for being the girls' favourite. He remembered those long talks towards the end of day or in the cab and fixing up the dates for Saturdays. He himself was surprised on how much he had changed from being a loner during college days, to becoming a guy, to easily get mingled with and enjoying the company of friends. Sometimes, he thought to himself it may be because he missed Sunny and wanted to keep himself engaged. This was an unnoticed change in his lifestyle. Life was work and fun, and there was fun at work.

During his initial days in the corporate world, he was frank with all friends and would crack jokes at any given time, especially during lunch, when boys had lunch together and girls sat together in the next corner. They would often hear Manu and would laugh amongst themselves. Though Manu had his workstation surrounded by girls, he had to travel twenty to twenty-five days a month anyway, so whenever he was back in the office, he would join all his male friends.

It was towards the end of the financial year that the work pressures had been a bit lifted, and Manu's business travels had been reduced a little, so he was a regular at the office. One afternoon, when Manu was back after a coffee break, he saw to his desk Preeti, the talk of the crowd, who had pulled his chair next to Vandna and was seated and discussing something in a very low tone audible only to the two of them. When Manu reached his workstation, Preeti pretended as if not seeing him arrive and kept taking to Vandna in a hushed tone. Manu coughed a little as an indication that he was there and to make his presence felt and also to let Preeti vacate his chair.

Preeti saw him standing and apologetically, with a very sweet gesture, said, "Sorry to have taken your seat. Would you mind seating at mine? I have something urgent to discuss with Vandna." Before Manu could revert, she added, "Hope you won't mind." There was no alternative left for Manu, so he moved back to the side cubicle and sat on Preeti's workstation.

Girls make their workstation homely, and there were numerous items in them like some wish cards with some quotes, red ribbons, small glass artwork that may be from the Archie gallery, a pen stand with few good pens, a sticky note, a lunch box, small and big purses big purses, a shawl on the seat, and many small items still left uncounted. As he sat on the seat, he smelled some very feminine touch of fragrance. It was good. He could smell the mild fragrance from the shawl on the back of the seat. He started to look at each and every item on the desk with keen interest again, this time trying to correlate the taste and personality of Preeti with all the items she had kept. It was interesting to note that the items kept were feminine yet displayed a classy taste. Finally, as he reached the tiffin, which was at the corner, he could smell the food kept inside. Maybe it was close to lunchtime, and he had started to feel hungry as well.

He was engaged in his thoughts when he felt a slight touch on his shoulder. He moved as if he just woke from a deep sleep and saw Preeti standing close by. The nostalgic fragrance, which was feeble when he sat on the chair, was quite deep now. He tried to get up but felt as if he was stuck to the chair. Preeti noted when she came that Manu was looking at tiffin and to extend the discussion, she just mentioned, "Manu, if you are hungry, you can have my tiffin."

"No, no, it's okay. My tiffin is about to come."

Boys used to have lunch from the tiffin service being provided by the nearby restaurant, and the food was good, but it had the same taste every day in all the dishes, dal or vegetables with those dry *chapatis (rolled Indian bread)*.

Hearing Manu reply with a "No," Preeti announced to all the other girls seated nearby, "Yes, why would have our food as your food comes from Keshav Bhai restaurant, and it has all the delicacy of dal, vegetables, roti, rice, salad, curd, sweets, and whatnot."

"No, that's not the case, Preeti."

"Then what is it?" asked Preeti in the same context.

"Okay, I shall share my tiffin with you today."

Lunchtime started, and today, Manu was missing from the boys' table. They thought him to be away for work and went ahead with their fast bite and then went out to stroll and smoke. Manu was amidst the all girls gang, and there were so many tiffin boxes opened on the round table. The Keshav restaurant had also given the delivery, and there were food in different colours and taste on the table, along with the chattering noise which made it difficult to understand who was talking to whom. Preeti was seated just next to Manu and asked him to try the dish she had prepared herself for her lunch. It was a *dum aloo* and was very delicious in taste. Manu tried to taste all the items on the table lest any particular girl felt less important and praised each bite with some good and funny facial expressions on which most girls would giggle and a few would just give broad smiles lest they may spoil their lipstick.

After the food, Manu shared a small piece of sweets with all the girls citing it as the "Keshav Bhai Prasad," and no one can refuse even if it can bring a slight weight gain in all the girls. Manu took excuse and joined his own male gang at the corner of Chandu Pan, their favourite place of hangout during office hours where they can ease work pressures that are surmounting. All of them were curious on where he was during lunchtime, and Manu narrated the whole story of the last hour and a half and also announced that tomorrow, his lunch would be at the girls' table.

"Leave it, boy. Don't get carried away, Come on ground (*Dharti pe aaja, abb jayada khawab dekhna band kar mere Bhai*) and stop daydreaming." It was Nishi who blurted it out. "Preeti is not the one to get fascinated by your mimicry. You do know the background story, so just chill and let go."

The next day when Manu was back at the office, he saw a card on his desk board. It was surprising to see who had given the card and pinned it to the desk board. He was glancing while setting up his laptop and settling his bag when Preeti walked to his desk and unpinned the card and handed it over to him. It was a friendship card with just "Hi" written on it.

Manu reacted to it by saying "Thanks."

"Just thanks?" was the reply from Preeti.

"Okay, you suggest."

"Not a big deal, but will you have lunch with me from now on?"

Manu thought for a while as all his friends would miss him, and he will miss all of them, but then he also remembered Nishi. *Okay, let me be with girls for a few days, and anyway, I can join them all at the Chandu Pan shop,* he thought to himself.

Manu confirmed, "Done."

Manu had proved Nishi wrong, and lunch with girls became a normal routine. Preeti would keep meeting him on some or the other pretext, and Manu also felt good in her presence. Preeti would find some or the other occasions to give beautiful cards and keep pinning them to his desk. Many a times, Manu thought to ask Preeti for a date, but his thoughts were left to himself. There were many meetings, picnics, and outings organised by the company, and Manu started to look forward to it, as it would give time for him to be with Preeti and spend some good time without offending any one.

The MNC had people development and teamwork high on their agenda, so the frequent meetings, celebrating big and small wins, appreciating the individual performance, reward and recognition, and many other extra activities had been part of their culture. A positive vibe always created a positive atmosphere, and bonding with each other gave employees a boost in working and developing an open culture, and this definitely supported the companies in their performances and a long-term commitment from their employees.

The team building trip was on the cards, and a few employees assigned on the task were engaged in selecting the dates, places, and making the travel plans. Though all this would be done by the event management team contacted externally, someone still had to share the brief outline and help them in coordinating the event with some details and the number of traveling members. The location decided was Kasauli, keeping in view the travel time and a beautiful location in the serenity of Himalayas. The team would travel from New Delhi railway station to Chandigarh by Shatabdi Express Train, and thereafter, Innova cars would drive through the winding roads to the location.

Everyone reached the railway station on their own arrangements in the morning. Manu was excited as Preeti was also part of his team travelling together. The team comprised of six females and five males. All the females were the daily luncheons with Manu, so there was all the more excitement and a lot to talk to which was left out during the office time's short breaks. Manu was on time, and so were the other team members. Preeti was a bit late, and as the time for train departure started to approach near, Manu could feel his heartbeat increase slightly for an unknown reason.

He took out his mobile phone and tried to reach Preeti, but her phone was not reachable. This made him more tensed, but he did not share his desperation to anyone around. Though the train would soon leave and everyone already on the platform have started to board the train, Manu kept waiting at the entrance. He went inside and kept his luggage in place and again came out to look for Preeti.

It was in the nick of time, and he could see Preeti coming out of the taxi. He rushed ahead to help with the luggage, and Preeti had made the extra payment in advance to cut down time. Manu picked up her luggage, and both ran towards the train which had already given the whistle and started to crept by. Both got inside the first compartment which was at the front and took time standing in the alleyway to catch their breaths from the short run mixed with fear of missing the train and thus causing inconvenience to everyone in the team they were with. Soon, they joined the rest of the group who were concerned in the beginning but later started to pass on the remarks that Preeti missed the train so she would have Manu. Manu just laughed it off and said that he was concerned as they were all travelling together, and she would have been left out had she missed the train.

The train had gained pace and everyone had settled. Manu and Preeti were seated next to each other and were still catching on their breaths. Manu had opened the newspaper to read, and then suddenly, he could feel Preeti placing her hand on his hand. This was the first gentle touch which made him sensuous and the blood warm around his ears. Preeti slowly whispered in his ear, "Thanks for waiting." Manu just smiled back and remained still lest Preeti would take her hand away. He wanted to freeze that moment forever as it was their closest moment, and he could feel her mild feminine fragrance.

She kept looking at Manu and also did not move; it was after a while when Manu realised that he did not want to make it public, so he kept his other hand on hers as a mark of assurance and then moved both his both hands. The touch had created a silencer effect on both of them, and they kept mum for a long time and kept sitting engrossed in self-thoughts. Preeti had closed her eyes and seemed to catch on sleep. Her head slowly leaned towards the shoulders of Manu and finally rested on it. Manu did not move so that Preeti can get the support and catch on some sleep undisturbed. He also felt good in that moment of closeness.

It must have been more than an hour and a half when the train came to a screeching halt at the station en route, and Preeti also woke up. By this time, everyone had rested, and that morning nap had covered the sleep gap and given them fresh energy. Breakfast was being served with a hot cup of tea, and the compartment, which was in a slumber just after the start of the journey from the New Delhi railway station, had started to buzz. They were served some eggs, some cutlets, and bread. It was a good break, and it was time to break their fast. Manu went with cutlet, whereas Preeti ordered for eggs purposely to share it as she had stared to enjoy sharing even small things personal or materialistic with Manu.

The railway steward had cleared the tables, and as the four rows from the back were all booked in teams, a few were standing and facing backward to have some conversations. Work discussions were over, and so they were generally either reminiscing the past team building or talking about how things would go in this trip and their plans for the three days ahead. Manu thought to take some time off and catch up on more sleep as breakfast had given him a bit of energy but also caused sluggishness. He slid a bit and pushed his chair back to create a head support and closed his eyes with his hands on the table. As he dozed off, he could feel Preeti gently placing her hand in his and turning his palm upwards. She kept moving her nails on his palm lines as if reading his destiny. Manu did not move lest he disturbs the moment of truth. This time, he was at ease, and her touch was pleasant and caressing. She even offered a slight support through her shoulder by straightening a bit.

The train had reached Chandigarh, and from there, they would travel in cars. It's not much of a distance; it was approximately forty kilometres, but it takes around an hour and a half due to the uphill drive and curved road. Also driving through the hills gave a nauseating feeling, and females are more prone to it, so they drove very slow and with halts after half an hour's drive.

Around noon, they had reached and checked in at Baikunth Resort. They transferred their luggage to their respective cottages. Manu and Preeti had adjacent cottages with a beautiful view of the ranges and the clear skies. One could see the hills and planes as far as the eyes could see. The sky was so clear, and it had a blue colour, unlike in Delhi or Gurgaon where it was hazy all around the year. After the baggage was stacked in the rooms, they started to take a stroll in the area to explore the other places, and finally, they got together at the lawns, which were another beautiful place with lush green lawns, spectacular and picturesque view, and great for basking in the sun.

It was time for lunch, and the event manager in charge had already directed them towards the area where lunch was being served.

—xxx—

The evening was spent paying a visit to a local town and a sunset point. The uphill walk to the sunset point was quite steep, and though the path was very decent being in the cantonment area, the climb was tough. Moreover, the corporates hardly exercise, so it was tiring, especially for the females.

Manu had been a great sport and a regular at the gym, so he had not much of a difficulty in climbing. He kept pace with others and did not to show his fitness and athletic gist. Preeti had started to feel tired in the first hundred metres, so Manu started to walk along and kept boosting, guiding, bending slightly forward, taking very small steps, and walking through the uphill climb. Preeti held on to his hand and put a firm grip, using his hand as a support and to help her ease the climb.

After around forty-five minutes of climbing, they had reached the hilltop, and it provided a beautiful view all around. One could see the multiple mountain ranges and the Himalayas covered with snow, with golden and white reflection from the setting sunrays. The other side showed descending hills followed by vast planes and rivers. On the horizon was the sun that about to set and was much bigger than its size during the day. It was just like a big ball of a shiny gold, disappearing into the dark shadows behind the skyline. Everyone wanted to capture the moment forever; some through the camera lens and others through their eyes and soul. It was fascinating. There was no corporate work pressure, only the cool breeze, pleasant sunset, a bit of chill in the hills, and the lovely company of friends. For Manu, it was all the more lovely being in the company of Preeti. He had started to miss her company most of the times now. He would find some or the other reason to be with Preeti, and same was the case with Preeti.

It was getting dark, and everyone had started to descend. By eight, the cars had reached the hotel gates.

The hill climb was tiring, but the weather and the lovely surroundings had overshadowed their tiredness, and they were all refreshed. They took a half hour break to get freshened up before heading back. Preeti was in the adjacent cottage to Manu and was ready in a few minutes. Manu had gone for a hot shower. He could hear his doorbell ring, and he just called from there, "Aye, who is this?"

"It's me, Preeti," was the reply.

"Oh! Come on in and have a seat. I will be ready in a minute."

She was hesitant a bit, but she came in and went over to the balcony side.

Manu had finished his shower and only had a towel on him. He came out with the towel on his waist, and Preeti could see him and his well-built upper torso, but she turned away to view the hills outside and deliberately diverted the topic, striking a conversation about the beauty of nature all around and the view outside, before Manu could take note of her seeing and mentally admiring his physique.

Manu was ready in his Friday casuals, and he put on his Denim Musk, his all-time favourite. He was ready to join the others on the open arena where the event management team had set the stage for the evening.

They left the room together, and because the path was a bit uneven, Preeti held on to the arm of Manu while walking through the pathway which led to the small lawns area. Most of the team had already reached the venue and were waiting for the rest to join. The place was lit very decently, and there was a bit of chill in the night under the clear skies, giving off a warm and cozy feeling of the place.

The light music in the background was soothing for the ears. The chairs were set in one side, with a small campfire lit in the center, and the attendant was offering drinks. The evening was great, and the gathering had become more open and the discussions had become more in pairs. A few were already on the dance floor while the others were watching from the outside and enjoying the moves. Kishan Kangaria ("KK" as he was addressed by his colleagues), the team leader, had already suggested for everyone to come on the dance floor and show their moves and also to enjoy the fun and take dance as exercise.

They all have gathered around the stage now, and almost everyone looked at Manu, expecting him to show them his moves since from his jovial outlook and always enthusiastic approach, everyone knew he was always a sport. During their last get-together, he had shown them his professional moves. Manu had attended dance classes a few years back when he thought that one earns in joining the film industry and becomes a hero in films, but the reality of life lands one in other avenues. Rashmi approached Manu with an extended hand asking him to join the dance floor, and Manu placed his glass on the corner of the table and joined her.

"Rashmi, we will have a set of moves on the dance floor. Let me get the song for you," Manu said to Rashmi and asked her to just wait for the change of the song. The song was for a female dance number, and it had them move and groove and twist and turn, and Manu performed his steps in time with the beats and asked Rashmi to join the sequence.

It was great to see Manu dance so perfectly and making female gestures and moves that the whole team was enjoying the moment. Rashmi would often topple while taking a turn, and Manu was prompt to hold her lest she falls down. One by one, all females kept joining Manu on the stage, and he would gladly help them with get their moves down on the dance floor.

Preeti had still been holding on to her glass and had not made any move. She had been silently watching the whole event and enjoying to herself, but it seemed she was somewhat jealous of Manu for dancing with other females in their group. She had been trying to shrug off the thought but could not get her mind out of it. Preeti was also a very good dancer, and on any other occasion, she was always the first to land on stage and hang on until the end. This was the first time she was just standing and watching others. It had been quite long and most of the team had already danced and left the stage to rest and refill their drinks when Manu approached Preeti and asked her, "Why are you not joining?"

"Just like that, a bit tired of the journey," she said, manipulating her words.

Manu held her hand and with the other hand took the glass she was holding, leaving it on the table. Together, they moved to the center stage.

He asked the DJ to play the number he had already advised.

The beats were on, and the thumping started. It was salsa.

Manu and Preeti looked a stunning pair and a perfect match for this type of performance.

The music was getting louder and setting the pace, and so were their moves. For fifteen minutes, they performed a continuous sequence of moves and thumping, and everyone was mesmerised by their dance performance.

The music finished, and they also took a break.

Manu was enjoying the dance so much that he did not want the dance to be over, and same was the case with Preeti, but they did not want to make their inner thoughts public.

There was a loud comment from KK. "Manu, we never knew you had these talents as well. I'm talking of the female dance performance. It was fantastic, man, and of course, the salsa was excellent.

Manu just smiled. "Thanks, boss, for the compliments."

Preeti had returned to the corner she was standing at before going to the stage. Manu also joined her there.

Both held back their glasses and took a chilled sip which was a good reliever post exhaustion of the dance. None spoke a word for some time.

Manu broke the silence. "You are awesome on the dance floor. Thanks!"

Preeti uttered, "And you too."

"Never knew you dance so well."

Preeti was standing and keeping her elbows on the parapet, and Manu could feel her breath on his arms which gave him a sensual feeling. He did not move for a while, and he realised that she was deliberately doing this. Manu could feel his arm's hair rising. He thought that if they had solitude, he would have planted a kiss on Preeti's lips that were so close to him now, but as they were surrounded by others, he just held her left hand playfully and tingled up her arm. She just reacted with a reluctant stroke back on his hand.

Everyone was slowly finishing their drinks and moving to the dining area, and only a few were left standing out and were into discussions. Preeti extended her hand with an empty glass and indicated for a refill. Manu took the glass and made two drinks for himself and Preeti, and he went back to the same place. He could feel that Preeti was already high but did not say anything while handing over the glass and indicating that all else had gone for dinner.

"I don't want this evening to end. It's so pleasant out here, and you are talking of dinner. We take dinner daily, but this time will never come back."

The chill was creeping in and Preeti was getting all the more closer to Manu. The place was vacant as almost everyone had gone and the waiters had started to close the dish bowls.

Manu made Preeti stand up, and both moved towards their huts. Upon reaching the door, Manu asked for the keys to Preeti's hut, but she refused and told him that she would rest and talk for some time in Manu's hut instead. Both entered the room, and while Manu sat on the couch, Preeti swung herself on the bed like how a log falls to the ground. A few minutes later while Manu was busy taking off his shoes, Preeti sat on the corner of the bed and suddenly got and came close to Manu. She planted a deep kiss on his lips. Manu was stunned for a moment but then held on to her and the smooch lasted a bit longer than usual. This was enough to break the barrier and that thin line in their relationship. He lifted her up in his arms and could smell the booze from her breath, and as he felt the depth in her inviting eyes, he slowly lowered her back on the bed, and both cuddled up under the bedsheet to explore the curves, contours, and depths of each other's bodies. They spent the night together and kept exploring new dimensions each time until the morning when Preeti left for her room through their linked doors.

The sun was shining brightly, and it was a lovely day with the team getting ready for the day's session. The event manager announced that after breakfast, there would be team building exercises, and post lunch, they will visit a famous local market.

The day was so fun with new learnings and out-of-the-classroom brain games, and the laughter and participation of everyone made it all the more rejuvenating. It was 3:00 p.m., and all were eager and ready to move to the marketplace just to hang around and feel the somber atmosphere there.

Everyone hopped into the cars and moved to the designated place. They kept the glass windows open to feel the freshness of the hills and breathe in the oxygenated air. Preeti sat in another car, and Manu had not been able to understand why, since that morning, she had been keeping a bit of a distance. He felt a little lonely inside, but he brushed aside the feeling and thought that it was just a female nature. They had not even spoken a word to each other the whole day long.

Upon reaching the market, they all got down and started to move in groups or couples as the road was not too wide. The shops were filled with local craft and souvenirs. Manu entered a shop and looked for something unique. He saw a hat that was designed for English-era female dignitaries. The hill town had a lot of English-era artifacts, and even the buildings belonged to the colonial times. He bought the hat and paced himself to catch up with Preeti who was walking alone. He opened the cover and placed the hat on her head. She was surprised to see the beautiful hat. She took it in her hand, admired it, and handed it over back to Manu.

"Why? It's for you."

"No. I don't wear hats."

"So what? No one here wears hats, but one can occasionally." Manu again placed it back on Preeti's head.

Preeti adjusted it and kept walking.

The hat had actually enhanced her feminine looks and everyone in the team admired her.

Everyone reached the hilltop cafe where the event manager was waiting for them to have their evening tea. They took their seats; it was an open cafe on the edge of a hill, and it had a beautiful open view. Preeti placed an order for coffee, and Manu took his usual his cup of tea. Preeti had been reserve in talking, the chirping was missing, and Manu was not able to understand this strange behaviour. He kept to himself and did not question her.

After a while, Preeti leaned closer to Manu and whispered in his ear, "Manu I need to talk to you."

"Tell me. Is there anything bothering you?"

Both got up from their seats, took their cups in their hands, and moved to the far end corner.

"Tell me," Manu said.

"Whatever happened last night, just forget about it."

"It's okay. But you trust me, right? And I love you."

"That's why I am telling you to forget it, and let's not cross the limit herein after."

"It's okay. If that's what keeps you comfortable, I am here for you."

There was a long pause and silence.

Manu was trying to understand what Preeti meant in saying that he should forget and not cross limits with her.

Preeti broke the silence. "My boyfriend, Sam Sukhwinder, is back from the United States. He has landed in India on today's morning after years of a short-term expatriate contract. He is a senior specialist in our company. He had texted me, but his message got delivered in the morning as there was scanty coverage here. He is coming to join me this evening. I don't want any hassle, so please . . . please . . . please keep distance lest you hurt him."

Manu was stunned for the time being. He could not believe what he was hearing. He remained motionless and could not find even a single word to respond to her. She removed her hat, placed it on Manu's head, said "Anyway, thanks for this beautiful gift," and moved on.

Manu took the hat in his hand and stood there for a couple of minutes still trying to regain and digest what Preeti had just said to him.

Everyone had moved and got into the cars and prepared to head back. Manu could feel that his feet had become so heavy that he had to drag them to reach the car. Once they were all in, they drove back to the resort.

Sam was waiting on the entrance. He was an inch more than six feet and very well-built with a fair complexion. He was also well-dressed, matching any Bollywood hero like Akshay Kumar.

Preeti was the first to get down and ran to meet him, and from the way they both met, it was evident that they were too close. All the team members knew him before, and they met and greeted him. Manu was the last to get out and reach the entrance.

Preeti introduced them to each other. "Sam, meet Manu, Manu, Sam. Manu has joined us few months back, looks after Site Engineering Projects."

"Nice to see you." Sam's hand was heavy like a hulk. Manu reciprocated similarly.

"Same here!"

"Okay, guys, see you at the lawns soon," Sam announced and left with Preeti to their room.

Manu was still in shock, and he dragged himself to his room. He was feeling sick and was unable to understand what to do.

Reaching the room, he went to the balcony and just sat there with an empty mind, not being able to think of anything. He remained there for quite a while, and then it was time for the evening get-together.

Manu thought to himself not to fall weak; he got up and went in to take hot shower. He spent a good half an hour there, and when he was ready, he was in control of himself.

He heard a soft knock on the door; he opened it to see Priyanka. "Hey, Manu, what makes you so late? Come, it's already time."

He followed Priyanka; she was a close friend of Preeti and also knew Sam very well. Both reached the lawns and could see Sam and Preeti with their drinks settled in the far corner. He avoided them and went off to catch a drink. Priyanka thought of giving Manu some company so as to avoid any scene after drinks, but Manu was not in to it.

He sat with Priyanka and coolly gulped his drinks. He had it more than the usual, and then he took leave from Priyanka and went off to his room and off to sleep.

In the morning, Manu was feeling heavy as he had a little more than the usual amount of drinks the previous night. Soon, it was time for breakfast, and they were leaving after lunch. He reached the restaurant to take some juice or fresh lemon water to sober himself; everyone in the team was already there taking breakfast, but he did not see Sam or Preeti. The feeling of aloofness was still lingering, and he was not able to come out of it.

He took his glass of juice and went off to sit with Priyanka.

"They are gone."

"Who?" Manu pretended to not know who Priyanka was referring to.

"Sam and Preeti. They left in Sam's car in the morning."

"Good."

"It's okay."

Manu could again feel the pang but tried to sound very normal.

Their cars had finally reached Chandigarh railway station, and all had got down. Mobile coverage was back.

Manu made few calls here and there. It was a Friday. The next two days would be available for him to rest and refresh.

On Monday morning, Manu posted his resignation mail to his boss citing personal reasons.

—xxx—

YEAR 2016

(Work, Reservation, Agitation, Effect, Some Suggested Solutions, and New Ventures to Move on To)

Two years into the start-up business, there was a lot to learn, and getting down to the very basic level had given them a very good insight on how various businesses are ran on a grassroot level in the Indian business scenario.

Every business, big or small, had its own share of start-up hurdles and learnings. With their growing confidence and towards positive finances, their mood had been in the upswing, but the drawback of this business house was the limitation of the time the business runs through the whole year. As the crop harvesting period runs for only four to five months throughout the year and all were free for rest of the year, it was not possible to survive with just one-third of the year in business period.

All were back to the brainstorming table to discuss and decide on the way forward and how best to put this time to utilisation and business enhancement. The suggestion had come from Adi, who said that as they were already into procurement and selling business, why don't they expand the same into controlled storage and selling during the period when apples are not available in the off season?

With all the discussions and deliberations, an agreement was reached in principle, but their partners would have to be given the entire knowledge of the gathering and a cost evaluation must be done before the final go signal, and only then shall the venture be enhanced in that direction.

The decision and work plan which seemed so simple and workable in this side of the discussion room was not that easy a task even after approximately two years of experience. The intricacies of the basics of storage had to be learnt, controlled storage houses had to be contacted, and financials need to be put into place. Although all the inputs gathered from the net and Google could not give too much insight, it was all still very helpful.

The state government had a policy to lease land for the purpose of construction and operations of controlled atmosphere storage, and it also extended subsidy under its policy. The land lease was cheap, but the overall investments required for construction and maintenance of the CA store were humungous, and to top that, the operational running cost was also very high. With few stores already set up in and around the apple belts and a few in the planes of adjoining states, it was advisable and evaluated that sharing the CA storage was the best available option as having your own CA store was a big and costly game altogether.

Setting up a CA store was also a very good business venture in long run, but even after the 70 percent subsidy from the state governments to promote the CA stores setup, it was still a very costly and time consuming investment. The quick and less costly method was to hire a portion in the existing store and store the yield in the combined and shared manner, and it was much cost effective.

Adi's sister Rubi and his brother-in-law had come to India from the United States. Mayank was a multimillionaire businessman well settled in the United States. On behest of Adi, Mayank was convinced on the venture they had started two years back. Adi had been enthusiastic as to how they have performed and had a positive outlook and growth. Mayank had shown interest to invest in the venture.

Adi, Sunny, and Manu were very excited to see Mayank's interest to invest in their small but steadily growing venture in India. Mayank had promised that when the next season begins, he shall invest a million dollars, which was a big money, and this would also give better returns and leverage in the market.

Coming from a well-to-do business family background, Mayank had received his college education abroad. At that time, only he had measured the differences and ease in doing business abroad especially in the United States and the difficulties faced in India. This was all due to the Indian government's unwillingness to resolve the unending issues in setting up the new business houses, so he had moved to the United States in the early start of the century. Now, he had established himself as a big business house in a decade's time and set up his own shopping complexes and retail chains which hosted each and every thing a person would need.

Adi had been asking his sister and brother-in-law Mayank to come and spend time in India as it had been a few years since they had trip there. On Adi's behest, Mayank had also agreed to spend time in India this time, as Adi was more a friend than brother-in-law or a brother of his wife. Mayank was informed that Adi had started a new venture which deals with apple trade and marketing business, and though he was aware of such practices in the United States, he had been only procuring them for his store and not storing in bulk as in the case of Adi's business venture.

Adi by now had his well-settled software and application development team who had been working together and getting orders from abroad and local clients. He had made his niche and had a very well-established setup. His company had been making decent profits every year, and his team had been growing steadily, but working with friends on an altogether new venture, he was feeling elated. He had been able to manage time for both the business fronts and software business which was mainly done online and on the phone.

The new venture had given him time to reunite with old friends, travel, venture into the wilderness, and explore the adjoining areas of Shimla where apples were grown; and even though staying close to the place, he could never spare time out of his business schedule to visit the locations.

It was fun to work, and outdoor visits made all of them feel refreshed and be filled with enthusiasm after every visit or meeting.

Furthermore, getting the financial investment assurance from his brother-in-law had all the more boosted his confidence and stature. The BMW, which Adi had always been dreaming of, did not seem a far-off dream now. He had been thinking of the models and which colour he would buy and whether to go for a complete down payment or through EMI; all such thoughts were flying through his mind whenever he was free. The excitement was building up and so was the work momentum.

Controlled atmosphere storage of apples: Apples are harvested just before ripening period and season and then stored in a controlled environment for months before being brought back to life and into the market when it is off season. There is a long history of postharvest technologies to extend the lives of apples. In the 1800s, producers exported apples from New York State to Europe in wooden barrels. The barrels were filled tightly with apples, sealed, and placed in the holds of old sailing vessels for their journey overseas. Months later, the apples were delivered firm and crisp.

Later, a new and similar kind of a cold storage system for apples was built in a room under the farm store, with a small natural spring running through it and a vent for warmer air. This keeps the humidity high and the temperature low.

In 2010, an apple storage was built which houses refrigerated storage as well as a room for controlled atmosphere storage (CA for short). Controlled atmosphere storage, a sophisticated technology, controls not only the temperature at which the apples are stored but the atmosphere as well.

In CA storage, apples are sealed in an environment that had around 2-3 percent of oxygen where temperature, humidity, nitrogen, and carbon dioxide are all carefully regulated. "Apples breathe," and as has been said, the deeper they breathe, the longer they'll live. The CA storage slows their breathing, which consequently slows their ripening and artificially makes the room perfect for the apples' long winter nap. Regular refrigerated storage is good, but CA storage is better.

Apples "breathe," and a controlled atmosphere storage slows their breathing, which consequently slows their ripening for a long time.

For farmers unable to afford CA rooms, there are other alternatives: a spray with an active ingredient, the 1-methylcyclopropene (1-MCP), which blocks the apples, ethylene receptors, and temporarily preventing them from ripening. It leaves eco-friendly apples, but they aren't certified organic. This spray biodegrades naturally and doesn't leave a residue. For farmers or associates, a cold apple storage in whatever form means keeping income coming in during the lean winter months. For apple eaters, it means being able to bite into a crisp, sweet apple nearly all around the year.

Apples are preserved inside the CA storage which may be used to extend the storage life of apples. The new technology, which entered the sphere, was called controlled atmosphere storage for apples. This technology has literally helped in storing the apples in a condition that their ripening process is stalled, and when apples are removed from the storage, the ripening process reinitiates. This keeps the produce fresh and crispy even in the off-season months.

The methodology is used so that different variety of apples can be stored at different temperatures, as apples are prone to flesh browning or physiological damage at slightest changes or may be caused by chilling injury. It is the utmost importance to know the storing temperature requirements for different varieties, which is generally -1°C to 0°C. TheAgricultural University Scientific Units has listed the storage temperature requirements for all the varieties produced in the region. In the CA store, the concentrations of carbon dioxide and oxygen mixture ration varies between

5 and 3 percent, respectively, depending on the type of storage.

Oxygen, which is primarily the factor for apple growth and ripening, is lowered and the room's door which is airtight is sealed. The room is flushed with nitrogen gas from an external tank to bring down the oxygen concentration to the desired level. It is desired that apples, after the harvest, are transported to the CA store immediately and as quickly as possible where the low oxygen atmosphere is attained. This will ensure that apples will be in a better quality even after the storage period is over.

Oxygen levels are continuously monitored and maintained by adding some more air to the CA store room when required and excess carbon dioxide is flushed out with nitrogen gas.

There are significant improvements made in establishing and maintaining the desired atmospheres. There has been a rapid increase in the use of air separators for the quick establishment of the low oxygen atmosphere. Computer-controlled automated systems are being used for analysis and control of the oxygen and carbon dioxide.

Use of 1-methylcyclopropene (1-MCP), an ethylene inhibitor, helps in the delay of fruit softening, yellowing, respiration, loss of treatable acidity, and sometimes the reduction in soluble solids, as well as development of some physiological disorders. The use of 1-MCP in combination with the CA system can further improve storability of fruits.

Precautions: The apples, which are to be stored in the controlled atmosphere should be checked for long shelf life and good quality. Apples which are raw or overripe are not good for storage. It needs to ensured that after the apple is harvested, it needs to be immediately transferred to the store, and it must be ensured that the room is rapidly cooled and quickly filled and stacked in the method devised.

The CA stores' atmosphere and the gas concentrations are controlled and not suitable for human life. If there is a need to do repairs or inspect any issue, it is advised to ventilate the room before and after working and then quickly reestablish the atmosphere.

CO_2 injury: If irregular, dry pebbly, sunken, or brown patches are observed on the apple's skin, it means that the concentration of carbon dioxide is high. This skin injury is further aggravated if there is a presence of water on the fruit. The three types of carbon dioxide injury is the formation of dark brown patches between the core and the skin, formation of cavities surrounded by discoloured patches, or suppleness without tissue browning.

Low oxygen injury: In such a case, apples become very soft and may even split open. The skin becomes bluish or purple, and the apple loses its crispness and flavour. The skin may develop dark brown patches or blisters in some places.

In both the cases above, it is recommended that prior to storing the apples in the CA store, there is a need to check the storing concentrations required for a particular variety of apples and keep it monitored from time to time.

—xxx—

It was February month of 2016, and other big business houses who had stored apples in CA stores had started to mobilise the manpower to start with removing and packaging the stored apples in the boxes displaying their company brands. Shipment to the major class A and B metro cities and towns across the country which are the main consumer points had also started.

The timing to mobilize produce to market needs to be perfect. If you get in to market too early, the normal long shelf life yield from the harvest and the one from the higher reaches of hills is still available, a bit too much delay, the big players flood market thus reducing the demand or destabilizing the market rates.

The decision was jointly made, to start the packaging by the first week of the February so that shipments could start to move out in the next week or the middle of the month. As scheduled, the first four truck shipments were out on the morning of February 16, and work kept progressing for the next three remaining shipments which got prepared and left on February 18, 2016.

The two of the four shipments had reached Delhi and got delivered; the other two were already on their way to Mumbai, and the last three left for Chennai. The transportation had to be through air-conditioned trucks and cold storage trucks, and it would take ten to twelve days for the shipment to reach the destination. After the produce was taken out of the store, the shelf life would get reduced. Packing had to be done very carefully, and each apple had to be handled individually lest to spoil it. One spoiled apple could ruin the whole basket in the transaction period itself. The trucks had been packed and departed, and the team got in touch with delivery points and drivers on the route.

On the early morning of February 19, 2016, there was a call from the driver of one of the trucks saying that they were stuck at Sonipat and unable to move ahead as people were on the roads and there was a lot of agitation ongoing and all roads were blocked. Even people have turned violent, and it was not known as to when the situation would be cooled down to allow them to move ahead.

Three truckloads had been stuck on the road, and drivers had parked the vehicles in whatever safest way they could do so and locked and abandoned the trucks.

The agitation had started on the ground by the Jat community who were rich, well-flourishing, and dominant people of the Haryana state, with the reason being the demand for reservation in government jobs and education system.

There was massive destruction of properties, shops were looted, roads were dugout, trains were halted, and chaos was all around.

The travel by roads or trains had come to a standstill. There was total inconvenience brought to the general public, but then, who cares, when these types of agitations are more politically motivated than being genuine in demand.

Mayank had discussed with Adi, Manu, and Sunny and decided to take the flight back to the United States. As all roads were blocked for the past week, he took the flight off from Chandigarh to Delhi and onwards to the United States with a promise to support them as and when conditions improve.

The trucks had been lying isolated for more than three weeks in the hot atmosphere. There was no contact with the drivers nor was there a location update.

—xxx—

***** SPACE *****

Every living or nonliving being occupies
space and survives and fights for space.

Financially rich buy their own space at a cost, and
the poor need to have protection for their space,
which can best be protected under democracy.

The whole fight is for space, and everyone is born
occupying the space God created, but the lust to
garner more space, bigger space, and if need be grab
others' space, starts the whole struggle for survival.

To ensure the poor have an equal right to space, the
need for reservations was felt long ago even during
the time when kings were the rulers and the world
was not fully discovered and there were no agreed
democratic norms of ruling or governance.

HISTORY OF RESERVATION IN INDIA

The reservation system was not new to the Indian context, and it had existed even before independence. The primary objective of the reservation system in India was to enhance the social and educational status of underprivileged communities and thus improve their lives.

Reservation system before independence: During the British period as well, there was a quota system which had favoured certain castes and communities. From 1882 to 1891, the princely state of Kolhapur, then governed by Maharaja Shahu, had implemented reservation for backward and non-Brahmin classes. During his regime, provisions were made to provide free education for everyone and ensure suitable employment. He appealed for a caste-free India and the abolition of untouchability.

In 1909, the British Raj introduced the element of reservation to the government of India in the Act 1909. In 1932, when the prime minister of Britain, Ramsay MacDonald, proposed a community-based representation where a separate representation was to be provided for Muslims, Sikhs, Indian Christians, Anglo-Indians, and Europeans. Under the provision, the backward caste and classes SC/ST and certain constituencies were reserved where they could only vote, although they could also vote in other seats.

The proposal was termed as controversial, which led to fast unto death, by Mahatma Gandhi who was, against it. The proposal was favoured by many from the backward classes, including B.R. Ambedkar, in the fear that they will not get fair representation in state affairs. An agreement by Gandhi was reached after negotiations, which agreed to reserve seats for the Dalits. The agreement came to be known as the Poona Pact, signed in 1932 in Pune.

Reservation system post independence: In 1954, after India became independent in 1947, 15 percent reservation was made for the SCs (schedule castes) and 7 percent for STs (schedule tribes) for a period of ten years and to be reviewed after the period. After the grant of this benefit, a caste-based reservation system became the birthright of those who got classified under this.

The major reform post the Mandal Commission report, which was submitted in 1980, actually got implemented in 1990 and listed 2,399 backward castes or communities, with 837 of them classified as "most backwards." The Mandal Commission report implemented in 1990 benefited some communities at the cost of many others.

The Supreme Court of India ruled in 1992 that reservations could not exceed 50 percent and that anything above which it judged would violate equal access as guaranteed by the Constitution. It thus put a cap on reservations. However, there are state laws that exceed this 50 percent limit. The Indra Sawhney case said that reservations in job promotions are "unconstitutional" but allowed its continuation for five years. In 1995, the 77th Amendment to the Constitution was made to amend

Article 16 before the five-year period expired to continue with reservations for SCs or STs in promotions. It was further modified through the 85th Amendment to give the benefit of consequential seniority to SC/ST candidates promoted by reservation. All these amendments are challenged in the Supreme Court, since these amendments altered the very basic structure of the Constitution and of the extensions being granted by all governments as no one wished to violate its vote bank and no government had been able to counter it.

All above cases and clauses are indicative that come elections Political parties become busy playing with the reservation policy, and by the time the Election Commission and the Supreme Court can act, basic damages of false commitment had reached the less educated and economically backward masses who were as always getting excited with false hopes in looking for a better future for their children.

The Gender-Based Reservation

The divide and rule system is no new in the spread of Indian politics. New means are always devised to keep voters in a frenzy so that they are not able to think and analyse the impacts clearly.

The upper house Rajya Sabha passed the Women's Reservation Bill in 2010.

There was a demand that reservation for women should be at least 50 percent as they comprised 50 percent of the population, whereas critics said that gender alone could not be held as a basis for reservation and other factors should also be considered. Economic and social conditions needed to be looked at, especially when educated and well-established women were applying for reservation. There was also a demand for women reservation in pre-existing reservations like the other backward classes (OBC), SCs and STs, physically handicapped, and so on.

In the state of Gujarat, 33 percent of posts are reserved for females in all government departments and services, such as police, health, education, and general administration, which had helped women in taking jobs in sectors other than education.

Religion-Based Reservation

There was no reservation granted on the basis of religion in the central educational institutions to religious minorities. Some states had been extending the reservation on religious basis and thereby altering the basic structure of the constitution framework. The government of Tamil Nadu extended a 3.5 percent reservation to Muslim and Christians respectively, reducing the cap of 30 percent quota of OBCs to 23 percent. Similarly, Andhra Pradesh introduced a law enabling 4 percent reservation to Muslims, which was upheld by the Supreme Court. The central government had listed a number of Muslim communities as backward Muslims, making them eligible for reservation.

Controversy on Religion-Based Reservation

The Prime Ministers Office (PMO) set up the Sachar Committee in 2005 to survey the socioeconomic conditions of Muslims while ignoring other religious minorities. This affidavit was filed in response to the Centre's stand that the scheme was valid and that the Modi government was to blame for the deteriorating condition of Muslims in Gujarat, whereas the Muslims in Gujarat are in better social standard compared to other states.

On May 28, 2012, the Andhra Pradesh High Court quashed the subquota. The court said that the subquota had been carved out only on religious lines and not on any other intelligible basis. The court criticised the decision: "In fact, we must express our anguish at the rather casual manner in which the entire issue has been taken up by the central government." This clearly indicated that the government had been trying to mislead people and creating controversial division for personal gains.

WHY JAT AGITATION

Surprisingly, a community that dominated every sphere of a state's life was crying discrimination. Jats was a community which was well-established and barring little percentages. They have maximum number of Members of Parliament, (MPs), Members of Legislative Assembly (MLAs), *zila pramukhs, pradhans, up-pradhans,* and they have dominance in bureaucracy, government, and private sector jobs and own the largest share in the state's irrigated land. With this stature, how can this community be called backward? The question of what exactly is the reason for the agitation in a peaceful state which had a good progress card arose, but it led to agitation which left twelve dead, vehicles and railway stations burnt, and the army deployed causing loss of hundreds of crore.

There were a few who had the required qualification but were unemployed. After getting a certain qualification, their mindset was made to believe that they were now eligible for a government job but not able to get one because of the reservation system, under which all jobs are taken by the reserved category, although that was hardly the case.

There were many educated, angry and unemployed young men, and those unable to find a job commensurate with their aspirations and education were amongst the thousands of protestors from a caste group that many say have no reason to protest but still took part of it as a form of support.

The Jats were the traditional landowners and were a powerful Hindu caste demanding classification as a "backward caste," a contention rejected in the previous year by the Supreme Court, so that government jobs can be reserved for them.

With the increase in population, the ancestral farmlands were getting divided and squeezed. On the other hand, most of the farmers were happy selling them off to get a better price from the builders which instantly improved their living standards. The next generation was left looking for a job. Those who opted to be engineers or took up other prominent professions did not have the corresponding English-speaking, analytical, or qualitative skills to secure a quality job to their self-satisfaction. The unemployment amongst the peer groups and individuals led to further resentment and thus venting out frustration at any smallest point.

On a deep dive, one could understand the various reasons as to why these protests were mainly getting towards the upper castes, socially powerful groups such as Gujjars from Rajasthan, Marathas in Maharashtra, Patels in Gujarat, and demanding for inclusion as lower castes were becoming more prevalent. Part of the analysis of employment data and evaluation of aspirations from few young Jats revealed that the protests were manifestations of India's slow, inadequate job creation, and a failing education system creating thousands of unemployed graduates. There were others who were lured by politically manifested agendas which made it evident that with unemployment being the reason, reservation was also a shield to political ploys.

There were specific and peculiar cases when one who scored a much higher percentage in the medical entrance examination did not get into merit, whereas someone with a much lower in score got to enter a government medical college only on the basis of being from a lower caste. The disparity in the fee structure between the government college and private college was so much that it was difficult for everyone to afford, and thus it raises a frustration level amongst the ones who deserved but could not get it because of the reservation system.

There were sectors which hosted contractual jobs and did not have any job security. Any illness on oneself or in the family history could throw one's life out of gear and impact the whole family's earnings. This being the major reason, protestors across India demanded to secure government jobs. There were times when the youth who studied to be engineers or doctors throng job openings for peons, clerks, and constables, and such was the case in Uttar Pradesh a few years back, when 2.3 million applied for 368 positions of peons.

A high income inequality, driven by a growing divergence between growth in productivity and wages, was the biggest challenge even as the quality of work and social inequalities based on castes and genders have been coming down gradually in the Indian economy. Employment data indicated two disquieting trends.

One, a slowdown in employment in the formal, organised sector (which in any case employed only 12 percent of India's labour force). In Indian factories, more than four hundred thousand people lost their jobs during the financial year from 2012 to 2013 as per the available stats.

The prime staging ground of Prime Minister Narendra Modi's Make in India programme had been successful to an extent but had not yet yielded the desired results as any such scheme implementation took time to bear fruits.

Two, this slowdown hid a larger, long-term trend: India Incorporations were automating and squeezing more output from its workers and so needs fewer of them.

In isolation, the latest government data show that the organised industry added nearly five hundred thousand jobs from 2013 to 2014. Unemployment in India, according to the labour ministry data, was less than 5 percent, but these data did not reflect under partial or disguised employment.

It was rationale to know that a monthly income of mere fifty-thousand rupees or more could put a person in the top 1 percent. Close to 82 percent of male and 92 percent of female workers in India earned less than ten thousand rupees a month in 2015. The seventh central pay commission had stipulated a minimum wage of eighteen thousand rupees per month. This suggested that a large majority of Indians were not being paid what may be termed a living wage, and it explained the intense hunger for government jobs.

The share of women workers in the lowest income bracket is 1.7 times that of male workers. Being a regular or salaried worker significantly reduced the probability of being in the lower income bracket compared to self-employment or contract and casual work. These trends persisted despite the fact that real wages grew across sectors between 2010 and 2015.

The number of unemployed youth was so high that the reservation alone could not solve the problem. The government, rather than addressing the economic stagnation and removing weaknesses in reservations through a consensus, recklessly expanded instead the list of beneficiaries through reservation inclusion.

The United Nations said India will have the world's largest youth population by 2020, and that population, in the age group of fifteen to thirty-four years old, grew from 353 million in 2001 to 430 million in 2011, with millions unemployed. What India needed annually was not just twenty-three or twenty-four million jobs but livelihoods.

As per the projected statistics, more than 250 million people would be looking for jobs over the next ten years as more women enter the workforce. This number had not taken account the people who would transfer from the agriculture sector.

It was obvious that job opportunities would come only with new investments and enterprises. If there is a need to create two million jobs every month, then there is also a need to create 20,000 to 50,000 new enterprises every month. At this stage of the business cycle, there needed to be a big push in the form of investment in infrastructure.

Timely envisaging the current and future fundamental steps taken by the present government, the target was to train a million people a week (400 million by 2022).

A step in the right direction was to improve the agriculture sector which catered to more than 50 percent related job market, with the efforts initiated by Modi Government for farmers such as the Fasal Bima Yojana, with an MSP of 1.5 Times, Soil Health Card, Per Drop More Crop, and the Kisaan Samman Nidhi Yojana with 6,000 rupees, wherein a minimum payment of six thousand rupees will be made to the small and marginal Indian farmers who have less than two hectares (4.9 acres) of landholding. Approximately 120 million farmers will benefit from seed purchase and other support. This definitely was the right step at the time when farmers had been leaving or were forced to leave the ancestral pride occupation for reasons beyond their control.

The two sectors which had seen growth and provided 1.4 million jobs were information and technology and telecom sectors. Secondary and tertiary sectors and the banking sectors had not seen any increase in employment which led to the fact that the government should focus on small and medium enterprises, revamp infrastructure, rationalise tax structures, revive skills in traditional industries, set up technical training institutes producing skilled workers, and ensure ease of doing business. Developing new skills and re-skilling older workers was a key approach, but there needed to be a massive skill development effort, which needed to do much more. The plan, massively ambitious in scale, aimed to train over 40 crore (400 million) Indians by 2022, which equated to approximately one million people per week.

This is a step in the right direction and is achievable with the kind of trust being given by the current government. Everything takes time to revamp. The thought process and direction is right, the approach and belief are in the right direction, the people's faith are all the time high, and thus, positive results are bound to come.

Gujjars announced, on condition that they will give up quota demand if Jats are taken off OBC list

There are communities who understand the complexities in the current scenario and the unreasonable demands on the reservation front which is based on the community rather than the economically backward class.

The state's backward communities within the other backward classes (OBC) group appear united against the Jats to demand their removal from the reserved category in keeping with a recent Supreme Court judgment.

The Rajasthan Gujjar Aarakshan Sangharsh Samiti has gone to the extent of announcing that it would give up the demand for separate quota if the Jats were taken off the state's OBC list.

Gujjars stated that they would not demand separate quota in government jobs and educational institutes if the Jats, who were never backward, are removed from the OBC category. The Jat community is very advanced and highly educated, as well as socially and financially dominant. This all shows that the agitation in February 2016 has not been for the rightful approach towards jobs or primarily against reservation but merely a reason to cause disruption which incurred losses to the tune of thousand crore. The deliberation is very wide, and there seems no end or outcome as any small change in the existing reservation system can be highly volatile to the government in power with a potential of aggravated outcome. No government can make even a slightest of modification if it does not have the will to do so and does not understand how it will benefit in the long run as the reservation was only meant for ten years' time and people would have to move from the caste-based to the socially and economically weaker sections.

Reservation: Understanding the Past and Present and the Solutions

The primary objective of the present-day Indian reservation system is to enhance the social and educational status of underprivileged communities and thus improve their lives.

The people live in a free country, and this freedom is a gift of democracy. The Constitution gives the right to freedom and most importantly to exercise this freedom in an equitable manner. At the same time, it is incumbent on the part of the state to ensure that equality prevails in all sections of the society.

However, in today's time, one of the major roadblocks to this equality is the caste-based reservation system.

India, being a developing nation, is facing many challenges, and the caste-based reservation system is one of them. The biggest question is whether implementing this reservation system has helped the downtrodden and the weaker sections of backward castes. The current scenario clearly depicts that the lower castes are still discriminated in their daily lives. To uproot casteism, it is important to fight the reservation system, which alone will lead to development, competency, equality, and unity.

The fact that people need to understand is that the present reservation system, which is purely based on the caste, divides the society. This is leading to discrimination and conflicts between different sections. This is the very cause of conflict of interests in a communal harmonious living.

Presently, in the government jobs and educational institutions, there is a reservation of 15 percent to the scheduled castes and for the scheduled tribes as per the government policy. Furthermore, there is a reservation of about 7.5 percent. Apart from the above, the state governments also follow their own reservation policies respectively based on the population status of each state divided on SCs, STs, and OBC basis. Hence, nearly 50 percent seats are reserved under the caste-based system.

The governments have been trying to modify the reservation system and for the same goal, the Mandal Commission was established in 1979 by the central government to identify the social, economic, and educationally backward classes. This was headed by the Parliamentarian B. P. Mandal and hence came to be known as the Mandal Commission. Its findings were that on the basis of caste, economic, and social indicators, OBCs (other backward classes) comprised 52 percent of India's population, so there should be a reservation of 27 percent given to them. This took the total reservation system to 49 percent with included SCs (scheduled caste), STs (scheduled tribes), and OBCs (other backward classes).

The report was completed in 1983, but in 1990, when the government of V. P. Singh implemented it, it led to countrywide protests from the students of all wings and resulted in self-immolation by students in large numbers. Thou there was temporary stay from the supreme court on any changes in increase in percentages but till date the reservation stands at 50 percent in all the states.

The very basis for the extension of the reservation system was to redress caste discrimination and uplift the people's social, economic, and educational status, on which it had miserably failed as these reservations were not utilised for these purposes and instead were carved for the benefits taken by the creamy layer under the reservation system.

As per the 93rd Constitutional Amendment, the government is allowed to make special provisions for the advancement of any socially and educationally backward class of citizens to support their admission in the government, semiprivate, or private institutions. The implementation of the reservation policy in the private sector has also been the point of contention in many forums.

The Article 15(4) of the Constitution empowers governments to make special provisions for the advancement of backward classes, and Article 16 provides the states equality of opportunity in employment or appointment in any post. The Clause 2 of Article 16 assures equality of opportunity in matters of public employment, and it states that no citizen shall be discriminated on the basis of religion, race, caste, sex, descent, and place of birth for any employment or office under the State.

The Clause 4 of the same article confers special powers to the states. The clause states that nothing in this article shall prevent the State from making any provision for the reservation of appointments or posts in favour of any backward class of citizens which is not adequately represented in the services.

There are two conditions under which reservations are extended:

1. The class of citizens is backward.
2. The said class is not adequately represented.

The above statements clearly state that **class** cannot be equated as **caste**, and caste cannot be the sole criteria to ascertain and declare a particular caste as backward (Balaji vs State of Mysore, AIR 1963 SC 649). Reservation should and must be adopted in advancing the prospects of the weaker sections in the society, but while doing so, care should be taken not to exclude admission to higher educational centers of deserving and qualified candidates of other communities. There are other prominent factors which need due consideration, and these are economic status, occupation, and place of habitation which may be in very remote or in tough terrains. These all need to be considered if the reservation is implemented in its essence. It further states that it does not mean that if once a caste is considered to be backward, it will continue to be backward for all other times.

The government is directed to review if a class reached a state of progress wherein reservation is not necessary. Hence, the government should remove that class from the backward classes list. In today's scenario, a class once granted admission to the reservation category can be taken in birthright and not allowed to be considered as advanced.

Though the Indian Constitution states that there is a provision of reservation to the backward class, nowhere has the term backward class been defined. This makes it very ambiguous to define backward classes as a backward caste, whereas the caste system has been the very basic structure of the Indian society, and castes were the basis of work division later formulated to create a divide under the British rule. Poor economic conditions were not caste specific.

The term backward class remained undefined, and only with judicial pronouncements over the period was it given some meaning which left a lot of room for manipulation by the political gambit.

Admission to any institution requires the mention of one's caste: SCs, STs, OBCs, or general. Based on this, the admissions to any institutions are accorded in priority. Merit comes secondary in one's selection or admission. There are many economically weaker children who are from the general category but cannot get the benefit of reservation by virtue because they were not from a reserved class. At times, children from the reserved class who do not deserve it still get the admission or appointment against a more capable candidate who is well qualified, and this causes resentment, which at times spurts out.

The economic status of the candidate may be the basis of granting reservation, but that too need a very intrinsic evaluation. Reservation should be extended once in a lifetime. Once the reservation is availed, the person should be removed from the reservation category list.

Everyone understands the need for all sections of the Indian Society to get an equal opportunity and be a part of the economy, but reservation based on caste is not the answer to this.

The reservation policy has been in India since independence. It initially started for a period of ten years and has been prolonged for seventy years at the whims of a lack of political will. To say if these policies really helped in uplifting the backward classes, there needs to be a revaluation.

The government should make education mandatory for everyone until the age of fifteen and provide all the support required for this. Under the RTE (right to education), lot of efforts have been made by the government, including the masses to send their children to school. A few states like the Himachal Pradesh wherein literacy rate is more than 90 percent have shown very good results, but other states like Bihar, Jharkhand, and Madhya Pradesh lag far behind.

Reservation is seen more as a vote bank than as a development tool. For reasons detailed before, the gaps in definition leaves lot of room to tilt the criteria which benefits the political party rather than being fair towards the growth and development of the national economy, and instead, it creates the disparity and differences in the society.

The reservation based on caste rather than those who do not have enough means of livelihood and those who cannot afford clothes and fulfill other basic needs for living is unfair and not acceptable. It is an antithesis of development and equality. Reservations based on castes or religion is not needed, but actually providing aid to those who have minimal resources and merit should be given equal and due importance in admission procedures as well as in employment opportunities.

Creamy Layer

The term creamy layer was first coined in 1975 in the State of Kerala versus N. M. Thomas case, when a judge said that the benefits of the reservation shall be snatched away by the top creamy layer of the backward class, thus leaving the weakest amongst the weak and leaving the fortunate layers to consume the whole cake.

The 1992 Indra Sawhney versus Union of India judgment laid down the limits of the state's powers: it upheld the ceiling of 50 percent quotas, emphasised the concept of "social backwardness," and prescribed eleven indicators to ascertain backwardness. The judgment also established the concept of qualitative exclusion, such as the creamy layer. The creamy layer applied only to OBCs. The creamy layer criteria was introduced at 1 lakh rupees in 1993 and revised to 2.5 lakh rupees in 2004, 4.5 lakh rupees in 2008, and 6 lakh rupees in 2013. Now, the ceiling has been raised to 8 lakh rupees as of September 2017. In October 2015, the National Commission for Backward Classes (NCBC) proposed that a person belonging to OBC with an annual family income of up to 15 lakh rupees should be considered as the minimum ceiling for OBCs. The NCBC also recommended the subdivision of the OBCs into "backward," "more backward," and "extremely backward" groups and to divide the 27 percent quota amongst them in proportion to their population and to ensure that the stronger OBCs do not corner the quota benefits.

Advances Under the Reservation System

The public sector jobs are divided into four categories: Class I (or Group A), Class II (or Group B), Class III (or Group C), and Class IV (or Group D). The Class I employees take up 2.2 percent of the public sector workforce, the Class II takes 3.3 percent, the Class III takes 66.8 percent, and the Class IV takes 27.2 percent.

For an Equitable Society, Should Reservations Be Extended to Private Sectors?

This is the demand being raised by the political sects who try to seek advantage by infusing temporary personal welfare agendas. There is a demand for extending the reservation into the private sector with the reasons solely to uplift the backward caste and not specific to the underprivileged.

These sects are not even ready to discuss the reservation system merits or demerits, but when they are approached, they have a completely different perspective. Their recommendations are to extend the reservation system in the private sectors as well. Their viewpoint is that there is an unholy nexus between the upper castes and the rich since long and keeping the backward classes, SCs and STs, suppressed and deprived. The issue of caste-based reservation has become a subject of conversation with many commentators calling for recasting or reviewing the system, whereas some are not even ready to discuss the matter at any cost. The suggestion for the category of the creamy layer to be introduced in the scheduled castes so that benefits of reservation can actually be extended to the ones in need is also a point of contention.

The prevailing reservation system is also responsible for the agitation of the Patidars in Gujarat and the Gujjars in Rajasthan. When Rashtriya Syam Sevak Sangh Chief Mohan Bhagawat issued a remark seeking a review of the reservation system, it was heavily opposed by the elite lower caste who were actually enjoying the perpetual benefits. Caste-based reservations has now become a concern of every responsible citizen, and reservations, if any to be, extended on the basis of economically backward class.

Most of the people crying foul over any discussion or alteration in current reservation systems are those who belong to the creamy layer of the lower caste. These are the people who are most effected. The creamy layer from the lower caste who received the potential benefits of reservation and happened to have studied in prominent technology and management institutions in India and abroad have become the custodian of the prevailing reservation system in India. For personal gains, they would ensure not to allow even any minor alteration lest it paves way for major changes in future. This shall extend the benefits to the actual lower caste that need the reservation for upliftment of their social status in society. Any suggestions or even a mere discussion on the subject of reservation are met with a strong opposition. They are prejudiced against any affirmative action for the socially oppressed, economically exploited, and politically marginalised sections of the Indian society. They want reservations in the public sector as well. It is nothing but an ideological position being proposed to ensuring equality, empowerment, and justice for all. But all does not include the above from the upper caste.

Who actually needs the reservation idealistically are those whose social and economic conditions are not good irrespective of the caste. The political setup continues to be a mute spectator for they are left with no tangible reason to sight the mammoth gap in job creation.

Exploitation in the Private Sector Because
of the Reservation System

In the year 2003, the telecom landscape was fast changing. Users were becoming aware and voice calls and cell phones were getting cheaper, mails and the Internet were making inroads to the Indian market, and the telecom sector started to witness steep growth. The way and at the speed service providers were working was not coping up with the consumer requirements, and the scanty footprint of the network was not even meeting bare minimum need.

The Infocomm "Monsoon Hungama" scheme offered multimedia phones at just 501 rupees, and the tariff rate of forty paise per minute had wreaked havoc on more than half a million people nationwide, which was a huge number at the given time. With very intriguing terms, customers were hooked on the network for three years, but by the time everyone realised, it was too late as the rerun path was much costlier.

The other big announcement in the changing landscape of telecommunication was the "Man Who Gave Away His Network," the tagline in the front page of *The Times Magazine* in the year 2004. A major outsourcing of manpower project had started.

The DPE (dollar per erlang) was the new buzzword. About 90 percent never knew what the heck this is and of the remaining 10 percent, the 90 percent never understood how to declassify. Nevertheless, it meant Erikson would make money on the basis of the deployment of the network.

Erikson, as the market leader, would take the major portion of the pie. The work and delivery war had started, the so-called war rooms were set, and they did not have bullets but bullet points. The pitch was always high, and project managers demand delivery based on the previous day's output. Chaos was being managed, and that's what Indians are experts at—creating one first and then enjoying and managing it later on. CC mails culture, ASAP execution, and SWOT analysis—the buzzwords had taken its precedence in the companies' working culture.

The private sector adopts social policies that are progressive and more egalitarian for all classes. The lack of employment because of the reservation for those deserving in the government sector lead them to venture into the private sector, where capitalists know the weakness of the system and are also aware of the salary structures in the government sector. The entry level where the major chunk of the workforce resides is squeezed in emoluments and incentives that make one feel down, but because there is no other option, one has to settle and compromise.

The working hours involves 24/7 around 365 days of the year. The operations demand round the clock working, and unlike the government sector which in such cases has a three-tier system, private sectors pull it with same manpower which disrupts the work-life balance to such an extent that one's physical and mental health gets long-term medical impacts. This is a one-way street, and if you don't want to work, there would be no problem as there are hundreds in queue to replace you and may be at a little lesser perks. Job opportunities are not easy here. Highly qualified masters and post-graduates apply for peon positions where thousands of applications are received, so how can the evaluations be done in such cases?

Reservation in South Africa

When South Africa got their independence from the British rule in 1990 under the leadership of Nelson Mandela, his supporters, mainly African tribes, demanded reservations in the education sector, government sector, and private sector.

Nelson Mandela replied that he will not allow any type of reservations in any sector, such as the in education sector, in the government sector, and in the private sector at any cost, because reservations and the products of reservations will destroy the whole nation.

The famous statement of Nelson Mandela is displayed at the entrance of the University of South Africa.

"Destroying any nation does not require the use of atomic bombs or the use of long-range missiles. It only requires lowering the quality of education and allowing cheating in the examinations by the students."

Patients die at the hands of such doctors.

Buildings collapse at the hands of such engineers.

Money is lost in the hands of such economists and accountants.

Humanity dies at the hands of such religious scholars.

Justice is lost at the hands of such judges.

The collapse of education is the collapse of a nation.

Above all, it creates a disparity in people living in harmony.

—xxx—

What is the government doing on job creation? Is it helping at a grass root level or is it just statistical?

The government started its skill development and PMEGP (Prime Minister Employment Generation Programme) and similar schemes. As per the data released by the Employees' Provident Fund Organisation, it shows that there are more than three million new jobs created until February 2018. The whole ecosystem that is building is such that people can find jobs for themselves and even become startup entrepreneurs. The jobs have been added, and now the looming concern is the quality, paying, and sustainable job employment.

Had the previous governments been hiding behind the reservation system and were not ready to take a rational call in time?

The reservation system has tagged even the most capable in the caste system as reserved instead of deserving. On the other hand, many reserved candidates in some categories are doing well in competitive examinations and scoring over the general category, but still, they are tagged under reserved category and thus impacting individual capabilities. Furthermore, anyone in the reserved category, when raised in the ladder because of their reservation, the acceptance by their colleagues is not well received. They may be forced to work in the official circle, but the acceptance is still not there in the social circle. If the changes are tweaked in the reservation system and a shift is made to a requirement-based reservation from caste-based, it will omit the difference and give them a much better chance to be socially accepted. The government hiding behind reservation shows its failure to generate employment.

Measures Being Taken By The Present
Government To Generate Employment:

> ➤ Skill Development Programme To Generate Employment
> ➤ Foreign Investments, Ease Of Business World Ranking Improvement, Improve Economy And Thus Generate Employment
> ➤ Pradhan Mantri Jan Dhan Yojana (PMJDY)
> ➤ Pradhan Mantri Mudra Yojana (PMMY)
> ➤ Pradhan Mantri Suraksha Bima Yojana (PMSBY)
> ➤ Atal Pension Yojana (APY)
> ➤ Pradhan Mantri Awas Yojana (PMAY)
> ➤ Sansad Adarsh Gram Yojana (SAGY)
> ➤ Pradhan Mantri Fasal Bima Yojana (PMFBY)

National Commission for Backward Classes (NCBC) 123rd Amendment) Bill, 2017. The bill was passed in the Parliament on August 2018.

What is the new amendment about? The Constitution (123rd Amendment) Bill gives the National Commission for Backward Classes (NCBC) statutory powers.

The present government revoked the National Commission for Backward Classes Act, 1993 and brought in the 123rd Constitutional Amendment Bill 2018 and the 102nd Amendment in the Constitution to make it a constitutional body. The bill passed will insert Article 338B into the Constitution after Articles 338 and 338A which deals with the National Commissions for Scheduled Castes (SC) and Scheduled Tribes (ST) respectively. The government proposed Article 338B which states that there shall be a commission for the socially and educationally backward classes to be known as National Commission for Backward Classes. The government proposal for the National Commission for Socially and Educationally Backward Classes should replace the NCBC was opposed by the OBC leaders, and the government decided not to change the prevailing nomenclature and continue with the status quo.

How Does Making the NCBC a Constitutional Body Help?

Under the NCBC Act, under India's Ministry of Social Justice and Empowerment established on 14 August 1993, the commission merely has the power to recommend inclusion or exclusion of communities in the OBC list.

The new bill allows it to look into all matters regarding the welfare and development of backward classes, as well as to investigate complaints. At present, the Scheduled Castes Commission, which looks into cases of atrocities against Dalits, is also in charge of hearing grievances from OBCs which mostly pertain to the nonimplementation of reservations in jobs and educational institutes.

The amended bill gives the Commission powers equivalent to that of a civil court. It can summon any person, ask for a document or public record, and receive evidence on affidavits. The most important inclusion of the clause is that the union and state governments will have to consult the commission on all significant policy matters affecting the socially and educationally backward classes.

The commission, which will have a chairperson, vice chairperson, and three members, will regulate its own proceedings. This will centralise the control with NCBC and refrain states from following their own exceptional reservation agenda.

Why the Bill Became Controversial

There was a very important step introduced. The bill makes the Parliament the final authority on determining the inclusion of communities in the OBC list and therefore **takes away the authority of states** which can now send requests to the NCBC, which, however, may or may not forward them to the union government. Until now, the NCBCs recommendations with regard to inclusions and exclusions in the list are binding on the government.

Lok Sabha passed the bill on April 10. However, when it was placed before Rajya Sabha, several members said that such an important constitutional amendment could not be approved without proper study. On August 6, 2018, as per the demand of the upper house, the bill was referred to a select committee. The bill was moved for discussion and passage by the social justice and empowerment minister in the Rajya Sabha and passed unanimously with 145 yes and no negative votes or abstentions.

After the passing of the new amendment bill, will this allow the NCBC the inclusion of Jats, Marathas, Patels, etc. who have been demanding OBC status?

The demands have intensified especially after 2010, when the OBC reservation was introduced in educational institutions. In 2014, in the wake of an agitation by the Jats in Haryana, Delhi, and Uttar Pradesh, the union government went against NCBC's decision and included the community in the nine states in the central List of OBCs, but the central government's decision was quashed by the Supreme Court.

With the new amendment, the Parliament gets the final authority to make changes to the OBC list; the NCBC would be able to take any call on the matter on its own. Thus, it centralises the change control in any reservation percentages, which were being manipulated by the state governments at their own whims during the spate of elections to woo the voters in their favour even after the Supreme Court's directions that there can be no surpassing the 50 percent limit. The states were just creating the fallacy in times and later backing out after causing damages and social unrest amongst the citizens.

A BRIEF HISTORY - THE INTRODUCTION OF OBC RESERVATIONS

The backward class of a citizen in Article 16 (4) can be identified on the basis of the caste system and not only on economic basis. Article 16 (4) is not an exception of Article 16 (1). Reservation can be made under article 16 (1). Backward classes in Article 16 (4) were not similar to the socially and educationally backward in Article 15 (4). The "creamy layer" is excluded from the backward classes. Economic criteria cannot be the sole identification criteria for inclusion to the backward class.

Reservation is provided to the scheduled castes (SCs), 15 percent, scheduled tribes (STs), 7 percent, and other backward classes (OBCs), 27 percent, through executive instructions issued and revised from time to time, which has been enforced in the law, as held by the Supreme Court in the Indra Sawhney case and is continuing till date.

The Kalelkar Commission, first set up in 1953, was the first to identify backward classes other than the scheduled castes and scheduled tribes at the national level. Its conclusion that caste is an important measure of backwardness was rejected on the ground that it had failed to apply more objective criteria such as income and literacy to determine backwardness.

The Mandal Commission Report of 1980 estimated the OBC population at 52 percent based on findings under three major headings—social, educational, and economic—and classified 1,257 communities as backward. It recommended increasing the existing quota of 15 percent and 7.5 percent, which were only for SCs or STs, from 22.5 percent to 49.5 percent to include the OBCs. A decade later, its recommendations were implemented in government jobs, a move that sparked major agitations and caused civil disturbance throughout INDIA.

To ease down the anti-reservation protesters, the P. V. Narasimha Rao government in 1991 introduced a 10 percent quota for the "economically backward sections" amongst the forward castes. The Supreme Court struck this down in the Indra Sawhney versus Union of India case, where it held that the Constitution recognised only the social and educational—and not economic—backwardness.

The apex court, however, held the reservation for OBCs as valid and directed that the creamy layer of OBCs (those earning over a specified income) should not avail reservation facilities. The overall reservation for SCs, STs and OBCs was capped at 50 percent. Based on the order, the central government reserved 27 percent of the seats in the union civil posts and services, to be filled through direct recruitment for OBCs. The quotas were subsequently enforced in central government educational institutions.

Institutions exempted from reservation:

The following institutions have been kept out of the purview of Central Educational Institutions (Reservation in Admission) Act, 2006:

Homi Bhabha National Institute, Mumbai, and its ten constituent units, which are as follows:

1. Bhabha Atomic Research Centre, Trombay
2. Indira Gandhi Centre for Atomic Research, Kalpakkam
3. Raja Ramanna Centre for Advanced Technology, Indore
4. Institute for Plasma Research, Gandhinagar
5. Variable Energy Cyclotron Centre, Kolkata
6. Saha Institute of Nuclear Physics, Kolkata
7. Institute of Physics, Bhubaneshwar
8. Institute of Mathematical Sciences, Chennai
9. Harish-Chandra Research Institute, Allahabad
10. Tata Memorial Centre, Mumbai
11. Tata Institute of Fundamental Research, Mumbai
12. North Eastern Indira Gandhi Regional Institute of Health and Medical Sciences, Shillong
13. Physical Research Laboratory, Ahmedabad
14. Space Physics Laboratory, Thiruvananthapuram
15. Indian Institute of Remote Sensing, Dehradun

The following institutions, though not specified in the Central Educational Institutions (Reservation in Admission) Act, 2006, do not have reservation in admission.

1. Shri Mata Vaishno Devi University, Katra
2. Birla Institute of Technology and Science, Pilani
3. LNM Institute of Information Technology, Jaipur

On October 27, 2015, the Supreme Court directed the state and the central governments to end the regional quota and to ensure that super speciality medical courses are kept unreserved, open, and free from any domicile status after the court had allowed petitions filed by some MBBS doctors.

Sachar Committee Report:

It reports that governments have been trying to befool minorities with quota: What is the government doing to address the issue of reservation?

In March 2005, the Sachar committee was set up to study the social, economic, and educational status of the Muslim community. The government did not publish the data as on one side, it did depict that the government is trying to befool minorities with quota, and governments should rather have a focus on providing basic amenities to them, and the report also indicated exponential growth in the Muslim population from 1961 onwards.

The report presented that minorities are promised reservation at the time of elections. It was further asserted by the committee that instead of making promises to give reservation, the government and its ministers should focus on the basic issues of improving administration and governance along with strengthening the education system for the backward section of minority communities. It is quite evident that even if the government provides reservation, the backward sections of minorities will not benefit from it because they are not in a condition to avail it. Hence, the government should focus on strengthening their education system and provide good governance.

Below is the graph, which depicts the population composition and growth rates:

Population Composition and Growth Rates (Percentage)								
	All	Hindu	Muslim	Christian	Sikh	Buddh	Jain	Other
1961	100	83.4	10.7	2.4	1.8	0.7	0.5	0.4
1971	100	82.7	11.2	2.6	1.9	0.7	0.5	0.4
1981	100	82.3	11.7	2.4	1.9	0.7	0.5	0.4
1991	100	81.5	12.6	2.3	1.9	0.8	0.4	0.4
Increase (1961-2001)	134	126	194	124	145	144	108	286
Annual growth (exponential)	2.13	2.04	2.7	2.02	2.24	2.23	1.84	3.38

* Data has been sourced

The committee recommended to set up an Equal Opportunity Commission to look into the grievances of deprived groups like the minorities. The aims are as follows:

- Create a nomination procedure to increase participation of minorities in public bodies.
- Establish a delimitation procedure that does not reserve constituencies with high minority population for SCs.
- Increase the employment share of Muslims, particularly where there is a great deal of public dealing.
- Work out mechanisms to link madrasas with a higher secondary school board.
- Recognise degrees from madrasas (local education schools) for eligibility in defence, civil, and banking examinations

The committee suggested that policies should sharply focus on the inclusive development and mainstreaming of the community while respecting diversity, but it has an inclined approach in its outcomes and suggestions.

The high population growth rate shall keep adding the numbers to the minority population and thus increasing the deprived state and inclined approach towards religious divide. The committee does mention that the prevailing reservation system does not reach out to the most deprived sections of the society, but it also does not suggest any measures on population control, and there were no recommendations by the committee in this regard.

The Republic of India (Bharat Ganrajya) is a "Sovereign Socialist Secular Democratic Republic" with a parliamentary system of government. The Supreme Court of India has described it as a "federal structure with a strong bias towards the Centre.

Weakest form of Indian governing democratic structure

Authority = Power + Legitimacy

In this sense of the term, nobody is supreme in India

as notion of supremacy derived from forms of power or sources of legitimacy of

SUPREME COURT, PARLIAMENT, CABINET, WITH THE PM AS ITS HEAD, PRESIDENT OF INDIA.

Forms of power and sources of legitimacy are varied and have varied hierarchy as per the individual's or groups' preferences.

1. If you believe in the authority derived from people, then the parliament or cabinet is supreme for you.
2. If you believe in the authority derived from the constitution and not from people (to have effective check on executive), then the Supreme Court is supreme for you.

In short, supreme authority varies as per individual and group preferences in the Indian context as it is not clearly mentioned in the Constitution.

Article 14 (Equality before the law): The sovereignty of the Parliament and the impartiality of the courts are free from governmental interference and the supremacy of the common law is applied.

Article 14 says that the state shall not deny any person equality before the law or the equal protection of the laws within the territory of India.

Article 14, the concept of equal protection of laws, is available to any person including legal persons viz statutory corporation, companies, etc. The concept of the rule of law is a negative concept, while the concept of equal protection of laws is a positive concept.

The concept of equality before the law is equivalent to the second element of the concept of the "rule of law." But certain exceptions to it are the president of India, state governors, public servants, judges, foreign diplomats, etc., who enjoy immunities, protections, and special privileges.

Article 15 (Prohibition of discrimination on the grounds of religion, race, caste, sex, or place of birth):

Article 15 says that the state shall not discriminate against any one on the basis of religion, race, sex, place of birth, or any of them.

Under Article 15 (3) and (4), the government can make special provisions for women and children and for a group of citizens who are economically and socially backward.

Article 16 (Equality of opportunities in matters of public employment):

Article 16 says that there shall be an equal opportunity for all citizens in matters relating to employment or appointment to any office under the state.

—xxx—

Government Announces 10 Percent Reservation for General Class:

The passing of the bill that set a 10 percent quota represents an important step and intellectual victory for caste reservations. Reservation as such has been seen as a roadblock by the upper castes till now, and the very basic structure of reservation on the basis of castes which were not helping the poor but putting a divide in the society has been opposed. The upper caste had the view and belief that jobs and educational institutions should only use merit as basis to provide reservation in

any form. The issue of the caste-based system has always been under contention by the upper castes as anyone being underprivileged but merely being from upper a caste was not given the reservation opportunity, thus causing the agony amongst all.

With the passing of the bill, upper castes also has a quota; it shall not be feasible to raise the argument as to merit be the basis of reservation. The bar set to qualify for the general category 10 percent quota is set so that huge numbers are going to qualify into this category. The 10 percent general category is not caste specific and caters to a holistic approach covering all religions. The bill was passed unopposed as no party could challenge it to displease the common masses, and thus it can be termed as a master stroke and intellectual win.

Ten Pointers On The 10 Percent Reservation For General Bloc:

1. Since the independence, governments have been trying to lure people by manipulating reservations as a goodwill gesture from their end, and the reservation system has practically lost the very basic purpose for which it was set as part of Indian Constitution framework post-independence.

2. Castes have been the fundamental building block of the Indian society since times immemorial but also the greatest source of backwardness due to many untoward reasons such as inequality.

3. The point to ponder and look at is if this 10 percent quota will benefit the upper caste, but it will need to be seen with time. However, this has definitely paved a way in bringing the socially

and economically backward in the category of reservation. The 10 percent quota which has been garnered for the upper caste is over and above the 50 percent limit set by the Supreme Court and does not barge in to the existing quota limits of other castes.

4. The 10 percent upper caste quota has been carved from the general block, and this is practically a subquota for the upper castes from the existing 50 percent.

5. Those who will qualify in the 10 percent general quota category is dependent on less than five acres landholding or 8 lakh rupees per annum income, which is so high that a vast number of members of the upper castes will qualify for it. It does little to make the situation on the ground better for upper castes but will surely pave a way for future discourse.

6. The inclusion of 10 percent additional quota in the current scenario ends the arbitrary 50 percent ceiling cap. The court offers little by way of explanation on where this number was pulled out. There is no law, anything in the Indian Constitution, or population statistics that back it up. The court simply states that there is a 50 percent ceiling. However, the 10 percent quota does open up new possibilities for those interested in backward caste advancement.

7. The Mandal Commission established in 1980 declared that 52 percent of the population comprised of what are today called "other backward castes." The 52 percent figure was based on the 1931 census data. It was predicted that the percentage would have further grown upwards as the birth rates in upper castes are relatively low. The 52

percent was over and above Dalits (17 percent) and Adivasis (8 percent), two other social groups who face social disabilities due to the caste system. These add up to 77 percent. The number of castes classified as "backward" has grown. When the Mandal Commission in 1980 identified backward castes, it listed 3,763 castes. However, as of 2006, the number stood at 5,013. One reason for the 2011 Caste Census data not being released by the Union Government is that "upper caste numbers are dangerously low," which will further lead to resentment if the reservation percentages are even slightly altered.

8. The numbers become manipulative and government-specific rather than justice-oriented, which means that the reservation system will keep prevailing and people will keep fighting amongst themselves, and the governments will be taking advantage of the divide. The blame on the upper caste having more quota or the lower caste not getting justice is ongoing, which needs a justice and judiciary end. With the increasing number of castes included under the reservation system and others raising their demands to be included, the time will come when 100 percent quota has to be divided on the basis of castes alone. This would allow for a community that lags behind severely to get a bit more of an assistance from society.

9. In the Indra Sawhney case, the 10 percent reservation for the poor, the court said that such quotas cannot be provided for poverty alone. It has to be poverty plus social and educational

backwardness, and the backwardness should reflect historic injustice through generations. The new bill paved way for the removal of the cap set by the Supreme Court.

10. With all said and done, the 10 percent quota represents an important intellectual victory for upper caste reservations. Though the upper castes have opposed the very basic structure of caste-based quota and insisted to be admitted based on merit, they also desisted the role of reservation to giving any benefit to the deserved than reserved. Based on this, upper castes always projected their legitimate right to where lower castes were being extended the benefits. Now that upper castes themselves have a quota, any argument based on merit will fall flat, as will any stigma around reservations. The intellectual argument has been settled so comprehensively that it has shifted the common sense of the Indian Union from opposing reservations. Now, even the upper caste interest groups have to settle for their own quota. It also needs to be understood that this 10 percen quota has paved a much deeper inroad to align the whole reservation system. Either this can lead to complete harmony or change whole existence of the system and puncture the bubble effect. With the NCBC's Constitution 123rd Amendment Bill, the government has practically ensured to give the powers towards central control and ensure that the new amendment of 10 percent reservation does not open inroads for the states to temper with existing percentages of reservation quota.

FORETHOUGHT

The Constitution (124th Amendment) Bill, 2019. The Bill was approved after the House rejected five amendments moved by opposition members. The Bill seeks to amend Article 15 to additionally permit the government to provide for the advancement of "economically weaker sections". Further, up to 10 percent of seats may be reserved for such sections for admission in educational institutions. The quota will be over and above the existing 50 percent reservation to SCs, STs, and OBCs.

As per the data available online and various surveys conducted, there are large numbers of vacancies lying vacant. There are more than one lakh positions vacant in the teacher's category itself, and other departments such as the police department have a vacancy of 4.43 lakhs. The number of vacancies vacant in the Indian railways has been more than 2.5 lakhs, and if all such vacancies are clubbed together, the total number of vacant positions will cross over 20 lakhs. This number is over and above the already existing workforce which has started to retire after their job life cycle.

The main reasons for these positions to be vacant are governments financial conditions and the additional burden on the exchequer. There has been a huge recruitment in past few months in the Indian railways sector, but this trend needs to be aligned in other sectors as well to improve employment rate.

India is the youngest country with a bubbling youth power, and this needs to be utilised in an effective manner, or else it will keep getting impatient and cause unwarranted disruptions on behest of few who have personal motives and find these energetic youth willing to do anything for want of money.

At the state level, the total budget that goes to pay the salaries of employees ranges from as low as 12 percent in Bihar and Uttar Pradesh to a reasonably high of 26 percent in Kerala, 25 percent in Rajasthan, and close to 30 percent in special category states like Uttarakhand, Jammu and Kashmir, and Assam. One of the richest states, Maharashtra, has 57.5 percent of the 2018–2019 budget going into paying salaries, pension, and interest payments, which went up from the 54.87 percent in the previous year. In the Defence sector, for instance, close to half of the Defence budget is already spent on salaries and pensions. The salaries are one of the critical components of budget expenditure.

With these kinds of percentages, it becomes all the more mandatory for the states to come up with a plan which will help generates independent employment solutions and skill development programmes started by the present government and will bear great results in the times to come. Not only shall this programme help in employment generation, but it shall also contribute to the growth of the Indian economy.

People look for employment as government jobs alone and reservation system are also applicable in the government sector as of now, whereas the private sector and entrepreneurs have been able to increase their earnings many folds comparatively. The other mindset, which is of a typical Indian, to get government jobs is for the security and it means less work. This has been very imprinted in the mindsets who work less and get paid well, which has been the case due to nonaccountability and evaluation. There has been a slight change from the time privatisation happened in most of the sectors and public sectors faced fierce competition from them, and when there came a need for survival, the public sector started to perform better. With the new government coming to power in 2014 and also getting through in most of the states, the accountability of each department was questioned, and delivery with timelines was asked for, resulted in a positive outcome, and supported in shrugging a lethargic approach.

In the present fiscal year, the Centre spent 1.68 lakh rupees crore in salaries, and pension expenditure is much more than that to the tune of 10,000 crore rupees. Filling up the vacancies is likely to add to the government expenditure. Nonetheless, the government, post the implementation of GST, had better tax collections in the kitty. After the reduction in global crude oil prices, the government did not reduce the basic petrol or diesel prices which has again given the benefit of healthy collections, and the same has gotten routed into the development of roads, ports, and other major infrastructure and nation building projects. In this eco cycle, this has also helped in creating the jobs and giving leeway to the government to fill up the vacancies which have long been vacant for want of funds.

The GST is divided into CGST (Central Goods & Services Tax and SGST (State Goods & Services Tax) and has supported the states as well. At the state level, the total budget that goes to pay the salaries of employees ranges from as low as 12 percent in Bihar and Uttar Pradesh, to a reasonably high of 26 percent in Kerala, 25 percent in Rajasthan and close to 30 percent in special category states like Uttarakhand, Jammu and Kashmir and Assam. One of the richest states, Maharashtra has 57.5 percent of 2018-2019 budget going into paying salaries, pension and interest payments, up from 54.87 percent in the previous year. In Defence sector, for instance, close to half of the Defence budget is already spent on salaries and pensions. The salaries are one of the critical components of budget expenditure. The central government, with a planned expenditure and implementation of new measures, had taken big risks and had started to show results. While keeping the inflation in control and all-time low, India's GDP is projected at a growth rate of 7.4 percent for 2019–2020.

Though the 10 percent reservation came in late, it still paved the way for the economically weaker and the so-called upper caste. Also, above all, it had broken the staunch myth of backward class quota, which is basically backward class manipulating the castes to causing all the disharmony in this big Indian continent with a large democracy and unity despite its diversity.

With these many open vacancies, the government must take steps to fill up the posts, which will smoothen the workforce on a grassroot level and thus boost the country's overall development along with creating new opportunities for a higher job employability.

Though class divide increased, social inequality decreased

Due to the mismatch between productivity and wage growth, there is a big inequality in income mainly in the case of workers. The wages in the workers' level have been growing at a much lesser pace compared to wages for the managers' level. Growth in labour productivity, which was always higher, experienced an even greater increase in the past fifteen-year period from year 2000 onwards.

The private employment sectors' approach is to employ managers who are able to squeeze maximum output from the workforce and make them increase productivity. For such cases, companies do not mind paying additional amount to the manager level as it takes off all the mental and physical load himself while the management is free to invest its time elsewhere more productively.

The new trend of contract employment which has crept in is a major contributor in the low growth of workers' wages.

While the overall wage productivity gap has increased, there is a good news on the gender inequality front. The aggregate gender wage gap has decreased both in the rural and urban areas for both casual and rural workers. As per statistics, women in the urban regular wage market earned 80 percent of what men earned. This value was around 60 percent in urban casual wage markets and both regular and casual wage markets in rural areas.

Gender inequality in earnings manifests itself differently across employment and educational categories. It is the highest in employers and self-employment categories and the lowest amongst regular workers and casual agricultural workers. In terms of educational categories, gender inequality follows a U-shaped pattern, with inequality being the highest for intermediate levels of education.

1. As per study, the lower caste groups are more skewed towards the lower income groups, and thus the Indian labour market is overrepresented there. The vice versa holds for upper caste groups.
2. It is well evident from the various studies till date that controlling the gap in education has been leading to narrowing the gap in caste-based inequality in earnings.

From the above two points, governments take the statistics of the first, and rather than bringing consistent efforts on education, the reservation system is put forth, which is a deliberate attempt to misguide the youth in the wrong direction. With the schemes launched by the government in last few years, like the Sarva Shiksha Abhiyan – Sab Pade Sab Bade, have been instrumental in providing education to the very poor society. Before giving the opportunity to the kids under the scheme, parents who are in the labour class have to be taken out of the burden of education. They have to be motivated to send their wards to the school for basic education. The RTE (right to education) step taken by the government wherein every child should go to school at least up to the age of fifteen is commendable.

The government is helping in providing books, nutritious meals, basic medicine, and vitamin supplements, and time to time guidance shall show results in the times to come. As for the youth who is able to get the basic qualification, when he starts to understand that he falls in the reservation category, he becomes diverted and the channelized efforts get reduced for various reasons as he can see that even if he doesn't make high grades, he shall be score and secure better jobs compared to his other classmates.

Creating equality by the vice versa trend is doing no good but increasing bitterness amongst each other not specific to anyone in particular and thus leading to outburst at times.

Evidently, regular employment has increased, as is visible from the increasing number of subscribers in the provident fund, and other social security schemes denotes an increase in the share of regular employment in the Indian economy.

To defining what a regular job means, it is the share of regular employment in manufacturing, construction, and services on the basis of three definitions classified as follow: formal 1, simple regular work; formal 2, regular work with provident fund or pension, gratuity, healthcare, maternity benefits, and paid leave; and formal 3, formal 2 with a written contract.

Unemployment is found maximum amongst graduates and post-graduates. Although the less educated are able to find jobs, because of uncertainty from either side, they are unable to sustain it for long. The gap leaves one worried for the time until the next job is secured and thus living a life of uncertainty. There is a need to look into job creation and shelve out the reservation system to come out with a true picture, and for this, everyone has to come to an agreement and act collectively.

AN APPEAL/MESSAGE

TO THE PRESIDENT. THE INDIAN
JUDICIARY. MEMBERS OF RAJYA SABHA.
MEMBERS OF LOK SABHA. STATE & UT
HEADS. HEADS OF ALL RESERVATION
COMMITTEES OF THE REPUBLIC OF INDIA.

THROUGH THE PRIME MINISTER OF INDIA

Subject: <u>Regards and Reconsiderations in the reservation
system on the basis of caste.</u>

Honourable Sir,

This is our great privilege, honour, and pride that your
government has absolute majority in both the houses as of
now. You have already steered the country in a very positive
direction which has earned massive respect all over the
world and which is evident from the visible approach by all
the VETO Nations as well people of our country.

Your dedication to the upliftment of the poor and also
the development of the nation as a whole, economically or
otherwise, has yielded very high results which is evidently
visible in the GDP growth and the low inflation rates.

India, is very diverse country, be it in terms of geographical spread, religions, castes, languages, food, dress, appearance, and many other aspects, but we are all united as being Indian. It is very difficult to meet every citizen's diverse and personal demands. Some of the programmes have existed, and your current government, which has implemented many new programmes for the upliftment of all sections of society, is highly remarkable. The main concern that a citizen of India has been seeing is the percolation and assurance that the programmes are implemented rightly and reach the grassroots level of society, which shall have tremendous impact on the overall upliftment in times to come.

Respected Sir, you implemented very successful programmes like Make in India, Swachh Bharat Abhiyan, demonetization to check corruption, GST implementation, OROP, and many such programmes with the latest one being the surgical strikes giving a clear message that India will take no nuisance and which have changed the Indians' outlook towards Indian politics. A lot needs to be done and everything takes time. As the saying goes, "Rome was not built in a day."

One of the main reasons India has not been able to reach the top League of Nations even after seventy years of independence is the caste-based reservation system.

It is well known that the reservation system was implemented for an initial period of ten years, and we all would agree that it would have been the need of the hour that time. Now, after seventy years, it has become a showstopper in India's growth. The highly talented youth when they don't find respectable jobs and when they are superseded by less qualified person, demoralizes them, and they plunge to seek opportunity abroad and thus leading to "brain drain" and benefiting other countries with the Indian trained and educated talents.

The caste-based system has been misleading as it is dividing the Hindu religion sect and also paving way for opportunistic politics for personal gains instead of keeping a nationalistic approach.

There are a limited few who have benefited from the caste-based reservation system. The creamy layer has been taking the benefit, and the poor in the reserved caste are left deprived as they do not have the basic amenities to reach a level where they can take benefit of the reservation. POVERTY IS DEFINITELY NOT CASTE-BASED.

I am a very small person to make any suggestion but would like to share my collective view as I see that it shall benefit the interest of the nation as a whole and not in an any individualistic group approach. We, the citizens of India, have to rise above the mutual conflict and look for the holistic approach.

1. The Article 117 has to be completely dissolved and reconstituted as it gives way for the Indian **state politics to override the central government's agenda,** and a few states have even overridden the Supreme Court directives and cases pending for a long time, thus creating disharmony amongst the local levels.
2. Doing away with a caste-based reservation system in education and on the job promotions, wherein people

feel it is directly **linked to financial benefits, and others who do not fall in the reservation category feel cheated** by the government's stand to continue with the existing system which is caste-based and is no longer proper after so many years of India's independence.

3. How much has the caste-based system in education and job reservation helped India and Indians in addressing the very basic essence for which reservation was formulated? Today, reservation in India in terms of caste is becoming a **birthright and a source of exploitation by the elite backward classes and politicians** to reap their own personal benefits.

4. The need of the hour is partly to build their election manifesto that we will do away with caste-based reservation system. They use it to empower those who are financially backward and also to align the reservation system in every bit that it helps in uplifting people's status from the grassroot level. Your recent step of giving a 10 percent reservation to the financially backward class has paved the way in the right direction, and it is the right step which shall benefit the poor irrespective of one's caste and religion. A two-way outcome is expected out of this. **One** is that is paves the way for the states to override the current limit of 50 percent as set by the court which shall further deepen the roots of caste-based politics and divide the country and the Hindu society. The passage of this bill could see regional parties raise the ante on reservation demands as they seek to consolidate their existing vote banks. During both the debates in the Parliament, almost every opposition, OBC or SC leader, while supporting the legislation, had voiced one common demand: to

raise the existing quota for the OBCs and SCs in sync with their population. **Two,** it is great step which shall help the poor who cannot afford to get the benefit even if they deserve it. In my opinion, this step indirectly acts as a catalyst in creating a reform in the current reservation system. The expected results shall be better with faith; we highly appreciate your first move which has been rightly timed and for the right set of people. Though personally, it does not benefit me, but this is definitely a very big step in the right direction from a nationalistic view that aims for "a victory for social justice."

5. The Constitution says "**other backward classes,**" and unfortunately, that has become **synonymous with other backward castes**. The economically backward section is a separate class altogether. Can this 10 percent be subsumed within the existing 27 percent reservation for other backward classes so that with all quotas combined, reservation does not exceed 50 percent? There has to be a balance between quota candidates and merit-based candidates, and also, it should not surpass the current 50 percent limit set by the Supreme Court.

6. **Accept any system in which the individual beneficiary's claims are considered and not a group's.** Whenever there are group-based benefits available to all members of the group, there is a vote-bank. Requirements must be formulated with an individualistic criteria.

7. Presently, there is a balance between the merit and quota seats. But if reservation exceeds 50 percent, it will become a problem as the number of people getting in based on merit will be reduced. If there is just one post,

there is a need to develop some criteria to select a person for that post. The criteria that the government chooses should be considerate of the individual candidate rather than the group to which he belongs.

8. We should device a way to stop putting caste names in front of our names in government documents, or else, the caste system will never end.

9. Removal of disparity—State Governments for the Political gains appointing contract employees and paying twenty percent of the wages against the same work for the designated post with equal qualifications. Fixing the contract periods are at the whims of the governing party. This is misleading and an exploitation of the masses.

10. Stringent social media control is required. Social media, though a boon in lots of ways, is being misused by corrupt forces not limited to Indian soil. Neighbouring countries take a sneak peek to jeopardise the Indian system and the economy by taking advantage of the country's diversity.

11. For the reservation system: incorporate abolition of the caste-based reservation system in the forthcoming elections and give a complete action plan to provide reservation for the following:
    a) Widows/Children of Martyrs - regardless of the rank he held so there can be equality in life and there is no disparity.
    b) Disabled - based on disability.
    c) Orphans - who have no support
    d) Financial Support for Poor Students - in a way not to encourage poverty

12. Do away with all subsidies. Slowly work in this direction so that people (our greatest asset) work and not survive on subsidy and spend time to create nuisance, which is counterproductive.

We see a great hope in you, who has the vision and the decision-making power to this Herculean task. We understand the reparations.

VANDE MATRAM

JAI HIND

SURAJ PRAKASH
CITIZEN OF INDIA

Stopping by Woods on a Snowy Evening

BY ROBERT FROST

Whose woods these are I think I know.

His house is in the village though;

He will not see me stopping here

To watch his woods fill up with snow.

The woods are lovely, dark and deep,

But I have promises to keep,

And miles to go before I sleep,

And miles to go before I sleep.

WILL CAST MY VOTE

I have never casted any type of vote in my life till date nor had I any strong inclination to join politics and do good for the nation and cast my first vote, but this time, I have decided to use my right to franchise.

This is my self belief that to contribute towards nation building either has to have financial power to bring those changes which one believes in, that by implementing these changes shall help in building of nation. The big industrialists or entrepreneurs are contributing towards nation building by raising the economy of the nation and thus making the country stronger globally through better quality export products and internally increasing the life standards of the people and thus contributing towards the overall development of the nation.

Or one needs a political or authoritative power to implement changes that can steer the nation into the right direction, but before an authoritative change can be implemented and can start to bear the results, one has to have the will to do so. But even before all that, there has to be a rightful and nationalistic thought and belief, and only then the whole nation can be further transformed. All this need a lot of sacrifice, and the first challenge is to rise above family bonds and attain the level of self-sacrifice. When politics is taken to garner self-interests, which is generally the case today in most political parties, the national interests take a back seat.

Their aims are to divide the society and to have personal gains. We are a nation with such a huge diversification in all respects yet remain united despite of diversity, but pursuing individual interests or community-specific interests is creating a division in the society.

In person, I never had much update on Mr. Modi's ideology. Coming from a Defence background, I never had much time to indulge into politics, so I have always kept myself equidistant from all political parties. My knowledge is limited to no more than what is in the news which I have read from the papers or seen on television.

When you took over the reins around 2013, I started to get a little interested on your nationalistic approach touching the very basics of the ultimate national interests. Your gentle, relented, nationalistic fervour is unmatched and truly not visible in the present political arena of any party.

The past five years have seen a tremendous change in the people's mindset. The nation has been seen standing united in a number of occasions. In your first address to the nation, you emphasised the need for Swachh Bharat. This has created a sense of self-pride to keep our place clean and country as a whole. There were many national level and international level programmes implemented for the development of the country, which have given paradigm shift the way people and political think tanks work. The works done for the upliftment of the common masses and the creation their self-pride is the reason that every citizen of India is standing by you today. From the many initiatives that were taken, a few has impacted the lives of the common man and some in particular are praiseworthy and could have been done much earlier to make them self-reliant.

Construction of toilets for the common masses: This has resulted in a cleanliness drive, hygienic living, and above all, living up to the dignity of females who were otherwise forced to use open spaces in unhygienic conditions before dawn or after dark, paving the way for all untoward incidents. This is a highly thoughtful action on the grassroot level for the common man to feel the first level of self-dignity.

The **medical insurance policy** at national and state levels is provided at the least possible payout and even free for the ones who cannot afford that small payment. It has also put the cap on the cost of medicines and the cost reduction in medicines or medical instruments which were far beyond not only for poor people reach but were even unaffordable by the middle classes. This has helped the masses in valuing human lives.

The **Sagarmala Project**, integrated with the development of inland waterways, is expected to reduce cost and time for transporting goods, benefiting industries and export and import trade. The project is mammoth with 150 initiatives with a total outlay of 4 lakh crore rupees, spread across four broad areas. It was an initiative of the Government of India launched in 2015, to enhance the performance of logistics sector in India. The programme envisages unlocking the potential of waterways and coastlines to minimise infrastructural investments required to meet these targets. Under the project, twelve smart cities will be developed near ports with an investment of 50,000 crore rupees. These will be integrated townships that will have affordable housing and implement green initiatives for sustainable living. The government has identified 1,208 islands for development along with 189 lighthouses. This is likely to boost both domestic and international tourism significantly.

The Golden Quadrilateral is a highway network connecting many of the major industrial, agricultural, and cultural centers of India. A quadrilateral of sorts is formed by connecting Chennai, Kolkata, Delhi, and Mumbai, and hence its name. The government has completed the Golden Quadrilateral highways project which connects the Delhi, Mumbai, Chennai, and Kolkata roads. Legal and engineering hurdles had delayed the initiative, which covers 5,846 kilometres between the four metropolises, after its start in 2000.

Statue of Unity: The statue is conceived as a naturalistic depiction of India's Iron Man Sardar Vallabhbhai Patel. It is the world's tallest statue with a height of 182 metres (597 feet). It is located on a river island facing the Sardar Sarovar Dam on the river Narmada. As the name suggests, the statue shall keep reminding all Indians that "we all stand in unity in diversity."

Foreign relations and trade: The foreign policy is focused on improving relations with the neighbouring countries in South Asia, engaging the extended neighbourhood in Southeast Asia and the major global powers. In pursuit of this, he has made official visits to Bhutan, Nepal, and Japan within the first 100 days of his government, followed by the United States, Myanmar, Australia, and Fiji.

Think India: From the nation's perspective it was important to improve relations with immediate neighbours as peace and tranquility in South Asia is essential for realizing the development agenda. There is an introduction of the concept of Para diplomacy in India where each states and cities would have liberty to forge special relation with countries or federal states or even cities of their interest. There is a bilateral trade relation with most countries except in few important global powers with which India shares a strategic partnership.

Strengthening the Indian Frontiers: India is deploying along its volatile border with Pakistan and other places, a smart Israel-developed fencing system having a "quick response team" mechanism, which strikes when the CCTV-powered control room detects an infiltration attempt. The BSF is implementing an ambitious project called the comprehensive integrated border management system (CIBMS) as part of the Narendra Modi government's plan to completely seal the Indonesia-Pakistan and India-Bangladesh borders in the next few years.

The BSF is tasked with guarding the two borders which are over 6,300 kilometres, and its chief, in an interview with PTI, said the new frontier guarding systems will bring a "sea change," for the first time in this domain. There is going to be a paradigm shift in our operational preparedness.

Navy set to open third Air base in Andaman and Nicobar Islands & Largest Naval Base at Karwar Commissioned: To counter China, the Navy will commission the new base, about 300 kilometres (180 miles) north of the capital, Port Blair. This will beef up surveillance of Chinese ships and submarines entering the

Indian Ocean through the nearby Malacca Straits. The facility, the third in the islands, will have a 1,000-metre runway for helicopters and Dornier surveillance aircraft. But eventually, the plan is for the runway to be extended to 3,000 metres to support fighter aircraft and longer-range reconnaissance aircraft. This is a strategical and a very significant step in enhancing the Indian presence and dominance in the region.

Buying Rafale Air Force: The Indian Air Force (IAF) is the loser in the war over Rafale. Nobody with even a rudimentary interest in national security will dispute that the IAF needs more firepower. At present, it has 600 combat aircraft and thirty-three active squadrons against a sanctioned strength of forty-four. We face two implacable foes on our western and northern borders. Any talk of a leaner and meaner military is met with shock and horror. It is a sad thing to say in the third biggest market for weapons (after the United States and China) that a nation that is building world-class rockets cannot build a state-of-the-art combat aircraft. The personal and political gains stooped low to an extent that the heat over Rafale has poisoned the chalice, and nothing will happen until after the general election. Once again, the IAF gets short shrift.

The current government has touched the grassroots level by providing the health benefits, gas connections for healthy living, toilets for hygienic living, electricity in the left-out villages, roads to every nook and corner, lowering the cost of medical expenses, directing subsidy in accounts of the deserved, the National Rural Livelihood Mission, enforcement of minimum wages, and the Mahatma Gandhi National Rural Employment Guarantee Scheme above all.

The rural housing Indira Awaas Yojana (IAY) and Pradhan Mantri Awaas Yojana (Gramin): This scheme provided houses to the poor in rural areas. The objective of IAY scheme was primarily to help in construction and gradation of dwelling units of members of scheduled castes and scheduled tribes, freed bonded labourers and minorities in the below poverty line category, and other below poverty line and non-SCs and STs rural households by providing them a lump sum financial assistance.

Universalisation of ICDS Scheme: The Integrated Child Development Services (ICDS) was conceived as the most viable vehicle for achieving holistic development with a focus on mothers and their child. The intended development of women and children, as a national priority, is being guided and pursued through the National Policy for Children. The target population includes pregnant women, nursing mothers, children up to six years of age, and adolescent girls. Supplementary nutrition, preschool education, immunisation, health checkup, referral services, and nutrition and health education are the main intervention packages offered under the scheme.

Breaking the deep-rooted judicial collegium, unwarranted foreign control of the fourth estate, biased CBI top brasses, nexus of forge companies, shell companies, *Hawala* money transfers, and many other concerns beyond the thought and reach of the common man. It was all a hand-in-glove relationship and so deep-rooted that it is beyond the common man's imaginations.

I would suggest to spend all positive balance funds on national building, and don't leave positive reserves. It will benefit your party to be back in power and rebuild the nation lest a new formed government will again loot the national treasure which has been made positive by your dedicated and untiring efforts.

The last BJP government from the year 1999 to 2004 did so many extraordinary works. To list a few, there are the nuclear explosion test, winning the Kargil War, roads development, education for all, making the national reserves positive but still lost in 2004 as the common man does not understand the nation building. Middle Class is too engrossed in self agenda of Tax and Top layer is for the Government which will benefit their interests but is very small number.

—xxx—

This is the writer's first book, trying to put his views which are thought-provoking in the current context of the Indian political system. The democratic setup, which is the preamble of the country, takes some nitty-gritty requirements to plug the gaps that are being politically exploited for personal gains by the people taking the system for granted since so long ago. The current political setup which get mandated to work for the country and the people of the country, if voted out of power, do not have any responsibility or accountability in the goof up done by them during their regime. The next government is busy implementing their own agendas, but there is a saying that you can fool a few people a few times, many people many times, but not all the people all the times.

The writer's first write-up was published in the *Indian Express* in the year 1984, when the newspaper had a column called "News from School," and the writer got a cash prize of twenty-five rupees.

The writer's second write-up was during the Naval tenure in Bombay, so called Mumbai in the year 1998, on the topic of INDIAN NAVY 2020. The write-up, though appreciated by the critics, never got published. It carried a cash prize of ten thousand rupees.

The Fifth Apple was written in the year 1988 but could not be made conclusive until 2018. The book is a faction (facts and fiction) and attributed to depict actual hardships, which come in a way for anyone who starts his struggle. The book takes back to the times before the country's independence to postindependence and the current scenario.

The writer has also shared some personal thoughts on the current situation, as to the willingness of the rightful leader and how the landscape of India is changing for betterment of country.

The writer has a personal love for the Gujarat state as it's the place which laid the basic foundation of his career path wherein he spent best part of his boyhood, four years into training in electronics engineering. Not that he considers any state different in India, but every region has its own charm, and that has created one's special love for it.

Jamnagar has been the writer's most favourite place, as well as Teen-Batti, the best junction he has ever come across. The nostalgic feeling of the area where the first thing he did was to step out and sit in a tea bar, a shop with loud music, and the tea had the flavour and the quality unmatched, with the cup upside down on the saucer. He sipped the tea and enjoyed the thirty minutes of sitting there.

He still remember his first landing in the Gujarat state. He took a train from Bombay via Dwarka Express.

He landed at Jamnagar railway station, and he could see salt dunes all around, under the clear and pleasant sky and unpolluted air. The white and pink cranes in the shallow back waters of sea and the moist and salty winds extended a warm welcome to the region.

Having extensively travelled in Gujarat in the year 2002 to 2004 wherein it was instrumental to get to the telecommunication networks on the ground, he had personally been traveling during the development of roads happening at that time. He travelled from Surat and all the way to Junagadh to Abu Road via the road almost covering the entire state. During this period, he had personally seen the speed in the development works taking place, which changed the face of the entire state.

"I have decided to cast my vote this time."

—xxx—

It was March 10 when Adi got the delivery confirmation call from Chennai that the trucks had arrived there. Though the apple delivery had reached its location, the produce had become fluffy due to high temperature exposure and cannot be sold in the market. It was a big loss on the start of the business not because of the reasons attributable to work and ethics but the cause and reason highly inexpugnable. It was more the individual losses, government property losses, and human lives loss that were responsible for all these. The law enforcement in India being poorest had been exploited by mobs on behest of hidden masterminds who would instigate any movement at any cost on the might of money laundering and political gains and power retention. The newly formed government was put into the test of times by the power hungry nincompoops.

The losses were unbearable. All the earnings to that day had to be used to pay and compensate for the loss. It was painful to take the decision, but Adi, Sunny, and Manu had decided to quit for now and wait for the conditions to become business friendly.

Adi was back to his usual technology business, Sunny went back to support his father, and Manu had decided to open a school in the village to support the rural children with an urban education system. Adi and Sunny had agreed to extend financial support to set up the school wherein students from the community would not only be imparted education at par but would also be provided with opportunities for a better future by making them self-confident and helping them with overall personality development programmes. With this vision in mind, in April 2016, the Rising Stars Global School was started in a small building in the mountains of Himachal Pradesh. Manu had moved back to the mountains where the teacher was still waiting for him, and for that reason, Manu started a new school. Sonia had agreed to join him and help him in his new venture.

—xxx—

INDEX

A TO Z OF PM MODI DEVELOPMENT PROGRAMS

Mission Shakti: India's satellite strike in space is as significant as its nuclear tests.

A -

- 24 MH-60R multimission helicopters
- Ayushman Bharat (PMJAY) – world's largest government-funded healthcare scheme
- AIIMS – 12 New All India Institute of Medical Sciences
- Air strike in Pakistan on JEM Camps
- Accidental death, disability cover at 12 p.a rupees - Pradhan Mantri Suraksha Bima Yojana
- Adarsh Gram Yojana (SAGY) – Rural development program, and to build the nation starting from villages
- Aspirational Districts Programme - Aspirational District Programme for underdeveloped districts to ensure balanced regional development
- Aadhaar Bill - Targeted delivery of financial and other subsidies, benefits, and services

B -

- Beti Bachao Beti Padhao,
- Bullet train – Ahmedabad to Mumbai
- Bulletproof jackets and cars to the Army
- Black money - All external routes closed
- BHIM app – For digital transactions
- Bharat ke Veer – Fund-raising app for paramilitary forces

C -

- Corruption-free India
- Coal block – Increase exchequer on auctions
- Coal production – Meet the demand and supply cycle
- Crude oil – Alternate channels
- Char-Dham Expressway – For year-round connectivity to Yamunotri, Gangotri, Badrinath, and Kedar Nath
- Corrupt CMs in Jail – Taking the bold steps to curb corruption

D -

- Demonetisation,
- DBT - Direct Benefit Transfer is an attempt to change the mechanism of transferring subsidies launched by the Government of India. This programme aims to transfer to the people's money through their bank accounts.

- Digital India - Digital India is a campaign launched by the Government of India to ensure the government's services are made available to citizens electronically by improved online infrastructure and by increasing Internet connectivity or by making the country digitally empowered in the field of technology.
- Digital Payment – Great Push to go digital. Cashless India.
- Diwali celebrations in Ayodhya – Birthplace of Rama
- DigiLocker - Enables Indian citizens to store certain official documents on the cloud. The service is aimed towards reducing the need to carry physical documents and is part of the government's Digital India initiative
- Defence budget - Crossed 3 lakh crore

E -

- Ease of Doing Business - **India** improves rank by 23 positions in the **Ease of Doing Business**
- Electrify India / electrify every village - Saubhagya (2.5 crore houses)
- E-way bill system
- Enemy property paw – Custodian will be the authorised owner post 1968
- E-Tendering – Bringing fairness in working
- Education - Increased 10 percent seats in university and college,
- E- Rikshaw 2 crore,

- E-BOOKS FOR ALL STUDENTS UP TO 12th STANDARD, free and available online.

F -

- FDI increase $22 billion to $36 billion, foreign policy
- Fiscal deficit reduction from 4.8 to 3.5,
- Farmers –
  o Fasal Bima Yojana
  o MSP 1.5 Times
  o Soil Health Card
  o Per Drop More Crop
  o Kisaan Samman Yojana 6,000 rupees

G -

- General caste 10 percent reservation,
- GST implementation and waiver up to 40 lakhs
- GDP growth rate at 7.5 percent
- Ganga cleaning
- GEM – Government Online Procurement Portal
- GST for LIG houses - Only 1 percent

H -

- Home Loans - Cheaper at 8.2 percent
- Highway construction – Golden Quadrilateral
- Hindu interest for political parties
- Heart Stents – Capping the cost

I -

- Inflation control – 4.1-6.4 percent
- Internet charges
- IIT 5 New,
- IIM 6 New
- Indradhanush mission
- IT return speed,
- Insolvency and bankruptcy code,
- Income tax rebate up to 60 lakh revenue

J -

- Jan Dhan Yojana
- Jan Aushadhi Kendra
- JNU Expose
- Jeevan Jyoti Bima Yojana
- Juvenile Act

K -

- Kedarnath development
- Katra rail
- Kumbh as a world cultural heritage
- Knee transplant cost control

L -

- LED bulb price,
- Labour pension (six thousand rupees)

M -

- Make in India programme
- Mudra loan to 15+ crore
- Mobile manufacturers
- Mobile largest factory
- Maternity leave enhanced to twenty-six weeks

N -

- Northeast development
- NGO restrictions
- Naxal control
- NPA reduction
- NITI Aayog - National Institution for Transforming India

O -

- OROP – One Rank One Pension for Defence sector, long pending demand since 1971
- Open defecation-free villages (5.5 lakh)

P -

- Pradhan Mantri Aawas Yojana - (PMAY-G) 1.5 crore homes
- Passport ease and speed
- Pension Yojana - Atal Pension Yojana is a government-backed pension scheme in India targeting the unorganised sector

- Pregnant women – Welfare compensation of 6,000 rupees

Q -

- Quick loan (59 minutes)

R -

- Rafale deal
- Roads development
- Real estate price
- RoRo ferry in Gujarat and Varanasi
- RERA - Real Estate (Regulation and Development) Act, which seeks to protect home buyers as well as help boost investments in the real estate industry
- ₹Rupees payment – Agreement with Iran, with Russia in process.

S -

- Surgical strikes
- Statue of Unity
- Swacch Bharat
- Smart city – Development of one hundred smart cities.
- Startup India
- Standup India
- Suraksha Bima Yojana
- 104 satellite launch
- Skill India

- Stone Pelting Incident Reduction
- Solar Power
- Slaughter house closed -
- Sukanya Samriddhi Yojana
- Shell companies crackdown
- Sagarmala Project – 35,000-kilometre highways
- Self-attestation of documents
- Subhash Chandra Bose recognition
- Seaplane
- SWAROJGAR YOJNA

T -

- Toilets construction – To control open defecation
- No terrorist attack – High level security monitoring
- Trains - No unmanned railway level crossing in India
- Train coaches export
- Tax collection - Increase
- Taxpayers – Added post demonetisation
- Triple Talaq
- Tourism ranking – India becoming a tourist haven
- Tourist count – Increase in the numbers
- Tax rebate of 7.5 lakhs – Relief to working class taxpayers

U -

- Ujjawala Yojana (6 crores of LPG connections) – To poor households.
- Udaan Yojana – Cheaper and affordable air flights

V -

- Varanasi Development – Heritage town
- Vande Bharat Express - Train 18
- VIP Culture – Red beacon misuse curbed

W -

- Waterways – Kolkata to Varanasi
- War Memorial – At Delhi

X -

- eXposure – Hidden antinationals, secular "award Wapsi," "Tukde Honge" Gangs
- Extending no benefits – To family members

Y -

- Yoga Day – International Yoga Day on June 21

Z -

- Zero unmanned railway crossings
- Zero terrorist attack outside Kashmir
- Zero nonelectrified village
- Zero villages with open defecation
- Zero pilferage of subsidy
- Zero scam

—xxx—

A BRIEF FROM THE AUTHOR

The book is a fiction which draws some facts from the incidents occurred during the period mentioned and had caused quantum financial losses and even loss of lives, disrupting the peace in the whole region.

The agitation was more politically biased than actually demanding the inclusion of the Jat community in the reservation list and was only aimed to disrupt the newly elected government in the state. It brought people's lives to a standstill, instilling fear in the common man apart from causing the loss of properties.

The reservation system in India is a very deep-rooted system embedded in the government framework, and it does not only jeopardize the progress of the country but also cause disgruntle and animosity amongst the citizens of India. It is paving the way for manipulative politics, misguiding the public by giving them a false commitment, and enhancing the caste divide amongst everyone.

The purpose of writing this book is to share the holistic effects of the reservation system that are not only limited to government jobs but also extending its impact on the private sectors and entrepreneurs and thus causing disharmony in living.

The book also shares how the current government led by Mr. Modi has been able to rationalise and to a an extent helped remove the disparity from the reservation system by granting a 10 percent reservation for the economically weaker upper caste, along with a great move in the creation of new job opportunities.